For Mum & Dad, who teach a thing or two.

BEFORE YOU READ THIS BOOK, PLEASE READ THIS:

Everything in this book is totally true. How do I know? Because it happened to me, and then I went and wrote it down.

Signed by Kayla Grub, aged 12.

THE SECRET KAYLA GRUB

By The Very Real Kayla Grub Herself

Spelling corrections by Kate Eden

CHAPTER 1

Peach Perfect

'At last! Woo-hoo!'

That's me, bursting through our front door. I've just finished my last ever day at Peach Primary. Which means I'm now – like – totally grown-up! I won't have to wear this yucky peach uniform ever again. Yesss!

I fling down my schoolbag and do a victory dance, laughing at my reflection in the hallway mirror. Who cares? It's the start of the summer holidays. Boing boing – ha ha! Maybe I'm not so grown-up, after all.

Apart from making me look peach-ugly, Peach Primary was OK. In fact I was a star pupil: I have twenty-three certificates to prove it. How do I know it's twenty-three? Because my bonkers parents keep score and stick them up all over the house:

* On the fridge door: *Best Pantomime Villain.*
* Halfway up the stairs: *Best Leap from a Trampoline onto a Pile of Cushions.*
* By the toilet: *Best Use of a Glitter Gun.*

Wherever you look, there's a Peach Primary certificate for something impressive that I once did.

There's even a certificate for *Best Reaction to Coming Last in a Maths Test*. I can't remember how I reacted, but it was an award-winner. I've always suspected that the maths one isn't quite as good as the others.

I once tried to trash it by feeding it to Cleo, my cat. I tore it up into strips so it was easier for her to chew. But she kept spitting them out, and my parents caught me doing it. They wiped Cleo's spit off the paper strips, ironed them smooth, and glued them back together. Then they stuck the certificate to our front window, so the whole street can see it. 'Why shouldn't we show it off?' they told me. 'It includes the word "maths". Honestly, Kukoo!'

Kukoo is my baby nickname. My parents won't stop using it, no matter how many times I tell them. My grown-up name is Kayla and that's what I should be called, because I'm nearly twelve years old. Plus our postman told them that Kayla sounds like a princess, so you'd think they'd want to use it.

But even the maths certificate isn't fussed over as much as the trophy. I won it for *Best Attempt to Sing, Even Though You Can't Sing*. Mum polishes it every day and shows it off to her friends. 'They love hearing about my talented daughter!' she tells me, with a worrying lack of doubt. When these friends visit, I try not to be around.

This afternoon, my parents are waiting for me in the front room, bursting with excitement. To celebrate my last day at Peach Primary, they've made a special surprise. Only it's not a proper surprise, because earlier this morning I saw them giggling and trying to hide something in the kitchen drawer.

Time to poke my head round the door. 'Ta-dah! Clever Kukoo!' they sing, out of tune and very loud.

Here's what I see:

* A trophy-shaped cake.

* Twenty-three balloons, stuck to the ceiling.
  (They've actually numbered them.)
* Twenty-three party-poppers, lined up in a row.
  (They've numbered these too.)

I'm worried: this looks expensive. We never have much money because their jobs don't pay much, even though they work really hard.

Mum works in a restaurant kitchen, doing the washing up. She hates the greasy pans but likes being 'an independent working woman', as she describes it. Dad works in a teabag factory, sweeping the floor. He gets a bit depressed about it sometimes. But then he cheers up and says at least it's regular hours and he doesn't have to work night-shifts.

If I ever complain that we can't afford nice stuff, they tell me to be grateful that I've got a roof over my head, three meals a day, and my very own cat. Which is way more than lots of people in Olding, where we live.

Right now they're waiting for me to say something, so I act like it's a dream come true. 'Ooh! Cake! Balloons! Party-poppers! Amazing!' Then I can't help a squirm. 'But Peach Primary gives certificates to everyone. I'm nothing special.'

'Nonsense!' tuts Mum. 'Twenty-three certificates *and* a trophy! You're a genius, pure and simple. A future doctor or engineer.'

'Doctor or engineer?' splutters Dad. 'Why stop there? Kukoo's going to be Prime Minister of this great country. Or an astronaut. Or both!'

'Actually, I think I'd like to be a writer,' I begin.

But they don't hear me; they're too busy arguing about my future glory. 'Doctor or engineer!' shouts Mum, looking fiercely at Dad. 'Prime Minister and astronaut!' replies Dad, clenching his fists and glaring back at her.

I leave them to it and tuck into a mega slice of trophy-cake.

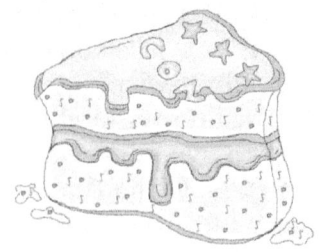

CHAPTER 2

Phone Call

They're still arguing (and I've started my third slice of cake) when – TRING TRING – Dad's mobile goes off. He scrabbles around in his workbag and fishes it out. 'Hello? Kevin Grub speaking.'

As the call drags on, he looks serious then worried. Mum and I watch him, trying to work out what's up. My mouth is still full of cake but I've stopped chewing.

Mum interrupts him. 'Kevin? What's wrong?' But he flaps her away and sticks his finger in his free ear, focusing on the call. 'Yes, I see. Thank you for letting me know.' He finishes up, then flops onto the sofa, all washed out.

Suddenly the house feels very quiet. I finally gulp down my mouthful of cake, but my throat has gone dry.

'I'm afraid it's bad news,' he begins. 'That was Granny Grub's neighbour, Mrs Handy. She says that Granny's very poorly.'

'Oh no!' wails Mum. 'What kind of poorly?'

'We don't know the details yet, but one thing's for sure: from now on, Granny's going to need someone to look after her.'

They reach out to each other and to me, and we have a full-on family hug.

Granny Grub is Dad's mum, and the best Granny in the world. When I was little, I used to call her 'GG' but she didn't mind. In fact that's what she still calls herself, sometimes. She uses my grown-up name, though: when I asked her to call me 'Kayla', she dropped 'Kukoo' straight away and never used it again.

I wish we could see her lots, but she lives in Newford which is miles away, and we have to save up for the train fare. So it's just Christmas and summer holidays.

'We can't afford to pay anyone to look after her,' says Dad thoughtfully. 'We're the only family she's got. It's down to us.'

I've got a feeling that everything's going to change – and not in a good way. I put the rest of the cake back in the tin, and stuff the party poppers back in the kitchen drawer.

'We can look after Granny ourselves,' declares Mum. 'We'll just have to leave here and move into her house.'

'But what about me?' I blurt out in a panic. 'In six weeks' time I'm meant to go to Orsum Academy, just around the corner! All my friends will be there. You can't send me to a school in Newford where I don't know anyone. You'll ruin my whole life and it's not fair!'

I know what you're thinking: I sound like a spoilt brat. And you're right.

But for some reason, they don't get mad at me. Instead Dad gently ruffles my hair, like he used to do when I was little. It makes it go all frizzy which is really annoying, because it's way too frizzy to start with. I do a big gulp to stop myself crying.

'Listen, Kukoo,' he says quietly. 'We know how hard it'll be for you to move away. But your Mum's right: we need to go and live with Granny. D'you really want to leave poor Granny all on her own?'

That's a tricky one. Of course I want us to look after Granny, but I can't bear to leave my friends.

I have one last go. 'Why can't she come and live with *us*?' I already know the reason, but Mum says it anyway. 'Think about it, Kukoo. This flat is barely big enough for you, Dad and me. Where would we put Granny? In the cupboard under the stairs? Granny's house has enough room for all of us.' I nod, trying to look wise and helpful but feeling miserable inside.

'Don't worry,' she tells me. 'We'll find you a brilliant school in Newford where you'll make lots of new friends. Orsum Academy isn't good enough for you, anyway.'

'I agree,' says Dad. 'Remember what happened when we visited? We didn't spot a single glitter gun or trampoline. And their last singing competition was years ago.'

He rushes over to the family laptop and taps away, looking for my next school. 'Bingo!' he cries. 'Newford has two schools, and they're right next door to each other. Which one d'you reckon, Kukoo? Swindel School or Clods College?'

'Swindel sounds a bit dodgy,' I reply, frowning.

'Dodgy how?'

'Isn't a swindle some kind of... trick?' I can't explain it. It's just a funny feeling.

'Nonsense!' he scoffs. 'Swindel School looks perfect. Just look at their badge with those super-shiny S's!'

To me, those S's look like snakes, but I've already lost the argument.

'Ooh!' he continues. 'Check out those snazzy blazers and caps!'

Mum nods heartily. 'That's the sort of top-class school our Kukoo deserves. Let's apply to that one!'

CHAPTER 3

Dear Swindel

Without stopping to think, Dad starts typing. He's so excited he bashes the keys too hard, which makes one of them stick. I work it loose with a paperclip, while he wriggles in his seat, impatiently.

'Honestly, Kevin,' sighs Mum. 'You'd save time if you weren't so hasty. Why don't you stop for a cuppa?' She heads to the kitchen to put the kettle on, but he glares at her and goes back to hammering at the keys. This is what he writes:

Dear Swindel,

My daughter will be joining your school this September, so get ready to welcome your new star pupil.

She's a future Prime Minister of this great country. But first she'll be an astronaut. To prove it, she's already shown talents with a trampoline and a glitter gun.

Yours proudly,

Kevin Grub

PS. She also sings.

'No way!' I wail. 'You can't say those things. I bet they only care about maths and stuff.'

'Nonsense!' he scoffs. 'They'll snap you up, and quite right too.'

But my point about maths makes him think, because he adds:

> *PPS. If you care about maths, then we have a certificate to prove she's the best person at coming last.*

He whacks the Send key and sits back in his chair, looking pleased with himself. But it doesn't last long. PING! Just a few moments later, he gets this reply:

> *Mr Grub,*
>
> *At Swindel, singing and trampolines are beside the point. I don't care what your daughter can do with a glitter gun. Only two things matter here: proper lessons and hard work. Coming last in any sort of test is simply not an option. Especially not in maths.*
>
> *In short, your daughter falls well below the standards expected at my school.*
>
> *Don't ever bother me again.*
>
> *Yours severely,*
>
> *Mrs Grimm, Headteacher*

Dad stares at the screen in disbelief. 'Surely there's some mistake?' he murmurs. 'She can't really mean it?' I want to shout 'Told you so!' but I know I'm not allowed, so I bite my lip until it hurts. Dad's desperate glance says it all: 'Kukoo my girl, let's enjoy these last few seconds before your Mum finds out.'

Too late: Mum walks in with Dad's mug of tea and spots Mrs Grimm's reply. 'Kevin, you idiot!' she howls. 'You've gone and stopped our daughter getting into the best school! How can she become a doctor or engineer, now?'

She bangs his mug down on the table so hard, the tea sloshes onto his shirt. Usually, she goes on and on about spoilt clothes, but this time she just stomps back to the kitchen, slamming the door behind her. I can tell how sorry Dad is, because he stays slumped in his chair, watching the tea soak through to his vest.

How has everything gone so weird, so quickly? Just an hour ago, we were a normal, happy family. We were celebrating my last day at Peach Primary. I was excited about the summer holidays and looking forward to starting at Orsum Academy in September. I had everything mapped out.

Now it's all turned upside down. Granny's ill, and we need to move in with her. Dad's got me thrown out of Swindel before I've even started. He's sloshed in a big brown tea stain and Mum's mad at him. Can things get any worse?

Yes, it's a mega-mess, but we still have one more chance. 'Hey Dad, aren't we forgetting something? What about that school next door?'

'Clods College?' he replies, like it's something nasty he's trodden in.

'Yeah, that one. Could we get in touch with them and word it a bit better? Gotta be worth a try?'

15

CHAPTER 4

Dear Clods

Dad's learnt his lesson. Before typing his next note, he spends ages fiddling with the paperclip and staring at the ceiling, getting the words just right in his head. He thoughtfully sips his tea, but they're only tiny sips because most of it's already spilt on his shirt. This time he taps the keys more gently:

> *Dear Clods College,*
>
> *Please can my daughter join your school this September?*
>
> *She's good with a glitter gun and that sort of thing. But if you want to teach her maths and stuff, I'm sure she'll be good at that too.*
>
> *Yours hopefully,*
>
> *Kevin Grub*

Mum creeps in and reads it over his shoulder. She must think it's a better note, because she presses Send then goes and fetches a clean shirt for him to put on.

As she hands it over, they exchange a look of pure love. Yuck! When my parents go all soppy with each other, I want to dig a big hole and hide in it. But I can't dig a hole in our living room, so I go back to fiddling with the paper clip. At least it gives me something else to look at.

The hours pass but there's no reply, and now we're all on edge. Mum twists her hair; Dad chews his pencil into splinters; I bite my nails and no one tells me not to. We all know how important this is: if I don't get into Clods, we can't go and live with Granny. She'll be all alone.

By bedtime, I've bitten my nails down to painful stumps. I'm just about to start on the skin around the edges, when – PING – a message lands in the inbox. 'I bet it's them,' says Dad. 'I daren't look!' says Mum. I try to sound casual but my shaky voice gives me away: 'Let's see what it says. Might as well get it over with.'

We nervously gather round the screen:

Dear Mr Grub,

Of course your daughter is welcome to join us! We look forward to meeting her in September.

Yes, we'll be teaching her maths and that kind of thing. But if she wants to bring her glitter gun, then even better. Here at Clods, we value every pupil's talents!

Yours helpfully,

Miss Pippa Skipper, Headteacher

We read it three times before we can believe it's true. Miss Skipper sounds way nicer than Mrs Grimm. And she actually wants me to join!

Mum's so happy she laughs and cries at the same time: 'Oh Kukoo, we knew you'd do it!' Dad swings me round in a hug: 'I always preferred good old Clods to snooty Swindel!'

They rush to the kitchen drawer and seize the party-poppers from this afternoon. 'Seems a shame not to use them,' chuckles Mum, clutching a whole fistful. 'Kukoo's earnt it,' grins Dad, grabbing what's left.

You wouldn't believe how much noise twenty-three party-poppers can make in a tiny living room. But Mum and Dad show what's possible. BANG, BANG BANG! (Plus the twenty other BANGS which I haven't written here.)

Cleo runs for cover, looking spiky because her hair's standing on end. The party-popper strings fly in all directions, turning the room into a tangled mess. Mum and Dad giggle like kids and I can't help smiling too.

Then I'm hit by a whole new problem. I feel bad spoiling their fun, but someone needs to say it: 'What about your jobs? If we go to live with Granny, where's the money gonna come from?'

Mum turns to Dad, suddenly serious. 'She's got a point, Kevin. We need to find jobs in Newford.'

'I know, I know,' he answers impatiently. 'But Newford's way posher than round here. We'll look wrong. We'll sound wrong. Who'll give us a fair chance?'

Now we're even more ridiculous: three people tangled up in paper strings, looking like the world's going to end.

CHAPTER 5

Job Seekers

Before any of us can think of anything useful to say, there's another PING from the laptop. We rush to the screen, trailing the paper strings behind us. It's a new message from Miss Skipper.

My whole world totters again: has she changed her mind about letting me into her school? Actually, no. It's a whole new miracle:

My dear Mr Grub,

I've just learnt some remarkable news.

Our Chief Washer-Upper, Miss Bubble, has won the lottery and is moving to Spain! Plus she's decided to marry our Assistant Caretaker, Mr Buckitt, and take him with her!

Why am I telling you this? Because we need to replace them before the start of next term. Do you know anyone suitable? A Chief Washer-Upper and an Assistant Caretaker?

Pippa Skipper

We can't believe our luck: these jobs are perfect for Mum and Dad.

'Quick, Kevin!' says Mum. 'Let's reply before she asks anyone else!'

'Hang on,' he teases. 'Shouldn't we slow down a bit? Stop for a cuppa?'

She's too worked up to see the joke. 'Are you mad? Just get on with it! Every second counts. Quick, quick!' She bundles him into his chair and flaps around him like a crazy bird.

He carefully begins to type:

> *Dear Miss Skipper,*
>
> *We can do those jobs! My wife Krystal likes nothing more than washing up –*

'Hmmff!' she snorts. 'As if!'

'I know, love. But we have to sound keen.' He hunches over the laptop and finishes the message:

> *She can bring her own rubber gloves and scrubbing brush, and I can bring my own overalls. Plus I'll be sure to wear my 'Fastest Floor-Sweeper' badge, to show I mean business.*
>
> *Do we get the jobs?*
>
> *Yours keenly,*
>
> *Kevin Grub*
>
> *PS. We'd work really hard.*
>
> *PPS. Do we get the jobs?*

'Dad, we sound a bit desperate,' I warn him.
'Well, Kukoo, that's because we *are* desperate.'
'Yeah, but we're not meant to show it!'

Too late: he clicks Send – and this time, the reply pings straight back:

> *My dear Kevin,*
>
> *Delighted for you and Krystal to have the jobs! I'll send the paperwork tomorrow. Or the day after. Or the day after that. (I'm usually a bit behind.)*
>
> *See you in September,*
>
> *Pippa*
>
> *PS. No need to bring rubber gloves.*
>
> *PPS. Ditto scrubbing brush.*
>
> *PPPS. Ditto overalls etc.*
>
> *PPPPS. All kit supplied at this end!*

So everything's sorted. Miss Skipper's done us proud: a school for me, and jobs for Mum and Dad.

Mum dashes to the kitchen to practice her washing up, humming one of her favourite tunes. Dad takes his *Fastest Floor-Sweeper* badge off the shelf and proudly pins it to his shirt. He even does a little dance, miming his best sweeping action.

The best bit is when he phones Granny with the news. 'Listen, Mum,' he tells her gently. 'You'll never be alone again. We'll be there to help you with everything.' I don't know what Granny replies, but it makes him smile and wipe his eyes.

I'm pleased for them, but I'm not celebrating yet. I'm going to wait and see how it all works out.

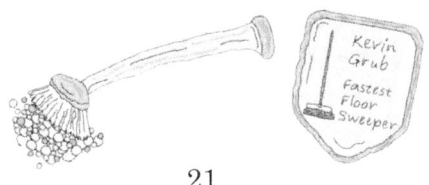

CHAPTER 6

Nearly Gone

The next few weeks pass in a flash: so much happens so quickly. But I'm still surprised when Dad rushes home with a pile of sacks from the teabag factory. 'They're for us to pack up our belongings,' he explains.

'But Dad, they're really smelly!'

'So?' he shrugs. 'They didn't cost anything and right now we need to save every penny.'

Cleo sniffs one of the sacks then goes off to hide in our manky old dustbin because she reckons it smells better. I take two sacks and pack them full of my kid stuff that I can't bear to throw away, even though I'm now grown-up.

With my glitter gun, I scrawl giant letters on each sack: KAYLA GRUB, AGED NEARLY 12. VERY IMPORTANT SACK. MUST NOT GO MISSING!

Saying goodbye to my friends is the hardest part. I give each of them a cupcake, bought with my own pocket money. My piggybank is now 100% empty and doesn't even rattle.

They promise to keep in touch, but they're already meeting up without me, even though I haven't left yet. Does that mean they weren't proper friends to start with? It's all so confusing.

Then a nice thing finally happens. I get a card from Granny, addressed just to me.

Kayla my love,

I know that things aren't easy for you right now. Of course you don't want to leave your friends, and the life you already know.

So I hope you don't mind if I share a little saying: 'every door has its own key'.

Once you get here, I think you'll find lots of exciting new doors to open. And I know you'll always find the key if you look hard enough.

Hugs,

Your very own GG.

Granny's right: I have to start looking forwards, not back. I stand up tall, straighten my shoulders and go off to check my sacks for the hundredth time. Anyway, there's no more time to mope around, because tomorrow's the day of our Big Move.

CHAPTER 7

Moving Day

On moving day, we're up early. Breakfast is just milk and a jam sandwich, because everything's packed away.

Dad's hired a creaky old van, which stutters up to our front door, bellowing dark smoke from the exhaust pipe. Mum folds her arms and rolls her eyes. 'Kevin, if we ever make it to Granny's in that thing, it'll be a miracle.' He starts whistling to pretend he hasn't heard. It's one of those times he looks desperate for a cigarette, even though he gave up years ago.

When we come to load our sacks into the van, they won't all fit. We try every way to cram them in, but each time there's one sack left over, sitting on the pavement. We're two hours behind schedule and it's started to rain.

Mum reaches into her handbag for her umbrella, then realises it's packed away in one of the sacks. Muttering an impressive list of swear words, she covers her head with a plastic bag. 'Will you stop messing with those stupid sacks!' she snaps at Dad. 'Just choose the least important one, and leave it behind!'

'Good idea,' he replies, pulling out a sack marked *Krystal's Special Clothes that She Never Gets to Wear Because We Never Go Anywhere Fancy*. He dumps it by the dustbin and squeezes the van doors shut. 'Right folks. Ready to go?'

Mum's speechless, so I say it for her: 'Dad, that's out of order!'

'Excuse me?' he frowns.

'You've ditched Mum's special clothes!'

'Yes, Kukoo, cos she never gets to wear them.'

'But Dad, don't you see? If you throw 'em away, it's saying that no posh things will happen to Mum ever again.'

'Well, they probably won't.'

'Eeuuuuwwwww!' That's the sound of Mum exploding with rage. She wipes the rain off her glasses and gives him such a glare, he realises his mistake. He reaches inside the van, pulls out a sack marked *Kevin's World-Famous Bottle-Top Collection*, and drops it into the dustbin. 'There it goes,' he groans. 'My pride and joy!'

I squash Mum's sack into the van before he changes his mind. At least this time, we can shut the doors. Without another word, we climb in and drive away.

Mum and Dad refuse to speak to each other for the whole journey. Radio? Forget it. Our only soundtrack is the cranky old engine and the broken windscreen wipers. One of the wipers squeaks and the other one plonks. Squeak – plonk – squeak – plonk, the whole way. It's enough to drive a girl mad.

I'm squashed in-between two sacks, and their lumpy bits are sticking into my sides. Even so, I manage to balance Cleo's cage on my lap. 'Hey Cleo,' I whisper to her. 'Don't worry, kiddo. It'll work out fine.' But she's still freaking out and who can blame her? This is a trip into the unknown.

By the time we arrive at Granny's, it's raining harder than ever. I jump out of the van, landing in a puddle that soaks through the hole in my trainers. On a normal day, this would be a major tragedy – but right now, Granny's more important.

I race to the front door and call through the letterbox. 'We're here!' The rain's running down the back of my neck, making me shiver. 'Hi Granny!' I shout again. Still no answer. That's weird, because Granny usually comes bouncing out of the front door in a big excited fuss. I wipe the rain off her front window and peer inside.

The sight's so shocking, I'll never forget it: Granny's asleep in her armchair, covered in blankets and looking tired. Next to her, the table's covered in boxes of pills and bottles of medicine. 'Shhh,' warns Mum, peering over my shoulder. 'Remember we need to be much gentler with Granny, now.'

'That's right', says Dad, getting out his door key. 'Granny's always looked after us, and now it's our turn to look after her.'

We softly open the door and tiptoe inside.

CHAPTER 8

Settling In

Over the next few weeks, we settle into our new family life.

Granny's house is so tiny, the rooms feel like shoeboxes. But Mum's right: our old flat would have been even worse. At least I still have a bedroom to myself. It's the little room right at the top, with a sloping ceiling that feels nice and cosy.

My bedroom door's the best thing of all: it's made of chunky wooden panels, carved with my very own initials. Granny did that bit herself, picking out the 'KG' in bold, daring swirls. Plus there's a little peephole in the middle. Granny fixed it up so it only works one way: I can peep out, but no one can peep in. It's like something out of a storybook, and I love it.

But the full-of-life Granny who made this door is long gone. Now she needs help with everything — even getting dressed, having a bath and going to the toilet.

Mum writes all the jobs onto a chart and pins it up in the kitchen. My jobs include brushing Granny's hair, filling her hot water bottle, and picking up anything she drops. I'm glad I wasn't given the toilet or bath job, but I guess I could do those if I had to.

Granny's usually too tired to say 'thank you', but if she's awake she reaches out to give my hand a gentle squeeze. Sometimes she dozes off with my hand still held in hers. When this happens, I perch on the side of her armchair, watching her sleep and feeling sad about her getting old.

I can't get used to how much she's changed. She used to be lovely and squishy to hug, but now she's gone all skinny, and I'm scared to hug her in case she breaks.

She's changed in other ways, too. She used to be the loudest, funniest person in our family. Bustling about the kitchen all day, cooking huge meals. Laughing so much it made her shake and wobble. Singing songs from when she was young, and making us join in the chorus. Telling naughty jokes and winking at me behind Mum and Dad's backs. Bursting with energy, ideas and plans.

Now she's so different: always quiet and always tired. When I look at her, I see a little old lady. It's a weird feeling.

'Do people sometimes shrink?' I ask Mum one day, when we're alone in the kitchen.

'Why do you ask, Kukoo?'

'Cos Granny's getting smaller.'

'Nonsense, girl. Don't be silly.'

But she's only saying that because Dad's just joined us and she doesn't want him to worry. She changes the subject: 'Only one more week of holiday, Kukoo. Time to start thinking about Clods College.'

I've been pretending that the holidays will go on forever. But each day, the truth is creeping closer: I'm about to go to a big new school where I have zero friends.

Dad smiles for the first time in weeks. 'Cheer up, Kukoo: your mum and I will be starting our new life, too. You're looking at two up-and-coming professionals!'

'Good point,' says Mum, still busy at the kitchen sink. 'Chief Washer-Upper and Assistant Caretaker! This is our big chance to show them what we can do.'

He proudly squeezes her shoulders, which makes some of her washing-up bubbles spill onto the floor. She tuts and pretends to be annoyed, then breaks into a big smile and hugs him right back.

Cleo clearly agrees with them, because she rushes in and paws at my feet. I know exactly what she's trying to tell me: 'Kayla, I know you're worried about your new school. But this new life isn't just about you; it's about your Mum and Dad, too. It's about looking after Granny and sticking together as a family. Try to remember that, to make the panic go away.'

At times like this, I reckon she's the wisest cat in the whole wide world. Just don't ever tell her I said so.

CHAPTER 9

New Uniform

The next day, my good intentions come tumbling down. All because of a stupid school uniform.

'Here you go, Kukoo!' announces Mum, pulling some shabby brown clothes and shoes out of her shopping bag.

My jaw drops in horror. 'You've gotta be kidding. I'm not turning up at Clods wearing that! No way!'

'What's wrong with it?' she demands crossly. 'It's the proper shade of Clods brown.'

'So what? It's way too big for me!'

'It gives you room to grow. It needs to last for years.'

'But it's already worn out!'

'It's simply second-hand. You know we can't afford to buy brand new. It took me ages to track it down, but I'm glad to say it was surprisingly cheap. So I've spent the extra money on ice cream for tea.'

'So I have the worst uniform ever, but at least we have ice cream? ICE CREAM?'

'Hey that's enough,' Dad warns me. He's heard me shouting and come to Mum's rescue. 'Clods is a school, Kukoo; not a fashion parade. OK, these clothes smell a bit mouldy, but I'm sure we can blitz that in the wash.'

I know I can't win. I tell myself that I won't eat any of Mum's stupid ice cream. That'll show them.

We get to tea, and Mum brings out the ice cream tub. 'How many scoops d'you fancy?' she asks me. This is my chance to show that I'm still gutted about the uniform. I'm meant to say 'Zero scoops! Zilch! None at all!' but of course I blow it. 'Any chance of three, Mum? Or even four?' 'Of course, love. Here you go.' Afterwards, Mum hands me the rest of the tub and I scrape it clean. Damn.

Now it's the last night of the holidays. Even Granny can tell how worried I am, because for once she's awake and watching me closely. 'You'll be fine,' she tells me. 'Step one, don't panic. Step two, find someone who looks friendly. Step three, just go up to them and say hello.'

'Thanks, Granny. I'll try.' Easy to say; harder to do.

I go to bed early. Mum has hung my nightmare uniform over my chair. She's tried mending the holes but it looks worse than ever. I cover it with my dressing gown and lie awake, thinking about tomorrow.

What do I know about Clods? The Headteacher, Miss Skipper, seems nice. But this town's way posher than we're used to. Instead of a teabag factory, it has a poetry festival. We're surrounded by people who look and sound like swanky TV presenters. We look wrong and sound wrong, just like Dad feared. What if I don't fit in? What if the other kids laugh at me?

Cleo jumps onto my bed, purring away. I reach out to her, desperate for her cuddly warmth. 'Hey Cleo, tomorrow's my Big Day. Wanna wish me luck? Any last-minute tips?' But this time, she has no wise words at all; she just wraps herself round my feet and dozes off.

CHAPTER 10

School Gates

I'm awake before my alarm goes off. Tomorrow is finally here: my first day at Clods College.

I put on my mud-coloured uniform and take a good, hard look at myself in the mirror. My sleeves are dangling down to my knees; my skirt's hanging wonky from my waist; and my shoes are so big, my feet are slipping around inside.

Just six weeks ago, I was happily bouncing around in my Peach Primary uniform. Now all I see is a ridiculous scarecrow. A little bit older and a whole lot sadder.

Cleo watches me through narrowed eyes that say 'D'you have to go out looking like that? Kayla Grub, this is an emergency!' When she talks like that, you can't ignore her.

I start by rolling up the sleeves of my jumper, so my hands poke out properly. Then I pull in the waistband of my skirt and fasten it with a hidden safety pin. For the final touch, I stuff balls of newspaper into my shoes, so they don't slip off.

What about my hair, though? It's sticking out in crazy directions, like a Halloween wig. I try to smooth it down, but this just turns it into a frizz-ball.

Cleo's eyes narrow to little slits of disapproval. 'You're right,' I tell her. 'I'm the school saddo. But you'll just have to love me, all the same. Cos right now, you're my only friend.'

Soon after, I'm hovering nervously at Clods' main gate. Crowds of kids are whizzing past me into the playground. They're wearing Clods muddy brown, just like me – only their clothes look nice and new.

I look up at the school sign. 'Clods College: We Try Our Best'. Someone's scrawled underneath: 'But You're Still Rubbish!' Who wrote that, I wonder? And why?

The sign is so wonky, it looks like it's about to fall over. It wobbles like crazy every time a car chugs through the entrance. Then a kid's bike knocks into it and – clunk! – it topples backwards into the bushes.

Ring! Rin–g! Ri–ng! R–ing! Ri–! R–! The school bell starts OK, but then splutters into silence. Doesn't anything in this school work properly?

'Hi there Kukoo! We've come to wish you luck.' Oh why did Mum and Dad have to follow me here? Have they no shame? What will the other kids think?

They're both super-excited about starting their new jobs. Mum's wearing her best dress, and proudly carrying her rubber gloves and scrubbing brush. Dad's wearing freshly ironed overalls, and his *Fastest Floor-Sweeper* badge is gleaming on his chest.

'Why did you bring your work kit?' I demand sulkily. 'Miss Skipper said not to.'

Mum breaks into a knowing smile. 'It shows we mean business, Kukoo. Two professionals at the top of their game.'

'Too right!' declares Dad. 'We're determined to prove ourselves. Nothing wrong with that, eh Kukoo?'

I'm so stressed-out, I finally lose my temper: 'For the millionth time, please stop using that stupid

Kukoo baby-name! This is a grown-up school and if anyone hears it they'll die laughing. I'm nearly twelve years old and my proper name is Kayla! And–'

They don't wait for me to finish. Mum nudges me towards the school. Dad's already heading to the staff entrance. I want to run home and hide, but Cleo would never forgive me. I take a deep breath, swing my bag over my shoulder, and go through the gates.

CHAPTER 11

Milly Mobbs

I start by traipsing through the playground, head hung low. Please - oh please - can I just blend in, despite everything? No one seems to notice me, so I finally lift my head and peep around.

One of the parking spaces says *Headteacher*. It's still empty and a group of kids have taken it over. They've dumped their bags and jumpers and are in the middle of a wrestling match – only it seems to be more laughing than wrestling.

A rusty old car pulls up into the space. The kids leap out of the way just in time to watch it drive over their bags and jumpers. But they don't seem surprised, so I reckon this happens a lot. The driver gets out and smiles at the wrestlers. She looks a bit old and tired and messy, but nice all the same.

'Morning, Miss Skipper!' shout the kids, rescuing their crushed kit from under her car.

'Morning, all!' she replies cheerily. 'Ready for the new term?'

'Yes Miss,' they laugh. 'Perhaps this time we might even learn something. Ha ha!'

Woah! That seems way too cheeky, especially for the Headteacher. But Miss Skipper just forces a smile, grabs her bag, and heads into school.

Why did those kids joke about not learning anything? It's a puzzle. But right now I've got more important things to figure out; I need to find someone to talk to.

'Right, Kayla Grub,' I tell myself. 'Remember what Granny said. Step one, don't panic. Step two, find someone who looks friendly. Step three, just go up to them and say hello.'

'Hi there!' I call out to a girl who's just strolled into the playground. She's pretty, with thick dark eyebrows, a glossy dark pony-tail and an all-round air of confidence. She looks ready for a fashion shoot, even though she's wearing Clods muddy brown like me. How does she do it?

'I'm Kayla,' I begin. 'Wanna chat?'

She takes one look at my wild hair, rolled-up sleeves, droopy skirt and extra-large shoes, then bursts out laughing. 'Chat with you, Frizz-Face? As if! You look like a dustbin. And from the way you speak, you sound even worse. Do me a favour: go find another loser like you.' She strides off into the crowd, leaving me all alone.

Oh Granny, you meant well but I wish I'd never listened. I'd rather be dead. This school is agony.

I'm still cringing with shame, when a new voice speaks up behind me. 'Couldn't help hearing that. If you're looking for another loser, here I am!'

I swivel round and find myself face-to-face with a girl who looks about my age. She's well-rounded, with long swishy hair that I'd kill for.

'You don't look like a loser,' I begin, shyly.

'Try me!' she giggles. 'You'll soon find out.'

'Err, ok.'

She takes my arm. 'Off we go then, Kayla. Two losers hanging out together.'

'Who's that other girl?' I ask her. 'The one who called me Frizz-Face and a dustbin?'

'Dunno yet,' she answers. 'I'm new here, too. But whoever she is, she's dead pretty.'

'And also pretty nasty.'

'Hey, you're funny! Where are you from, by the way? You sound so different.'

We soon get chatting. Her name is Milly Mobbs, but she says I can call her 'Mills'. She's a Year Seven, like me - only we're not really the same age because it turns out she's one week older. The biggest surprise is that she's got a twin brother, Billy, who's just started at Swindel School, next door.

'What d'you think of Swindel?' she asks me, looking through the railings into their playground. 'Pretty different to Clods, huh?'

All I know about Swindel is that their Headteacher didn't want me. It's a painful, awkward memory. But Milly's question makes me curious to find out more, so I peer through the railings too.

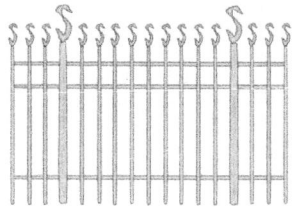

CHAPTER 12

Swindel Billy

Looking at Swindel, I realise that Milly's right: it's very different to Clods.

For a start, their sign isn't wonky. 'Swindel School' shines out in bright gold letters that dazzle. I still reckon those two S's look like snakes, but I don't tell her in case she thinks I'm mad. Beneath the name is the school motto: 'All Work, No Play'.

'No play?' I murmur. 'So they strip the fun out of everything?'

She doesn't hear me; she's too busy admiring the purple blazers and caps. 'Don't you wish we could wear that awesome colour?' she sighs. 'They make every Clods kid look like a mud-ball.'

'Or like the water in a washing-up bowl when it's rinsed too many dishes,' I add, knowingly. 'Although my mum says a good washer-upper always changes the water before it gets that bad.'

'Ha ha. You're being funny – again!'

'You're welcome!'

We look more closely at the Swindel kids. They're not laughing and tearing around like the kids at Clods; they're lining up in a long straight row, waiting to go inside. Shortest kid at the front, tallest kid at the back. No one's talking, because they're already reading their textbooks: huge heavy books with hundreds of pages. It looks like they're trying to memorize every word. They don't look happy.

A well-rounded boy nervously joins the line, fitting himself into the right height order. He looks just like Milly, but the boy version. 'Poor Billy,' she sighs. 'He's freaking out. Look: he's already got the Swindel face!'

It's true: beneath his jazzy Swindel cap, he looks tense and gloomy. He tries to blend in by pulling out a textbook, but he's holding it upside down without realising. In his other hand, he's clutching a musical instrument case, gripping it so tightly his knuckles stick out.

'What's in that case?' I ask.

'It's a banjo, Kayla. He's really good at it. A few weeks ago, he beat the Swindel kids in a talent competition. That's why the Grimbag's poached him.'

'The Grimbag?'

'Mrs Grimm, the Swindel Head.'

'You mean she *asked* him to come to Swindel?'

'Correct. When he wins the next talent competition, it'll be a Swindel victory.'

'And your parents agreed?'

'My mum's in charge. She says that Swindel will help to make him a lawyer, like her.'

'Why does he have to be a lawyer? Why can't he just be a banjo player?'

'That's exactly what Billy says. But Mum says that playing the banjo won't buy him any sports cars or skiing holidays. She says we're too young to understand.'

A horrible thought strikes me. 'Hey Mills, you won't have to go to Swindel, too?'

'No way! The Grimbag doesn't want *me*, cos I don't have any talents. I always wanted to play a musical instrument, but now I daren't try. What if I turned out to be good at it? I can't risk ending up at Swindel.'

The railings are like prison bars, separating Billy from his sister. He sneaks a glance at her and mouths 'Get me outta here!'

Someone else is watching him: a stern-looking lady, peering through a window above the Swindel main door. She's wearing a suit with pointed shoulders and a shirt with a stiff collar. Her shiny black hair's scraped into a tight bun, and her black eyebrows look fierce. 'Meet the Grimbag,' explains Milly. 'Doesn't she look a nightmare?'

So that's Mrs Grimm! I'll never forget what she said about me: 'Your daughter falls well below the standards expected at my school.' Those words still make my cheeks burn with shame.

A Swindel teacher comes out, blowing a whistle. The kids do a shuffle to make their line even neater, and shout out the school motto: 'All Work, No Play!' Then they march inside like an army, with the teacher blowing the whistle to keep their steps in time. Billy gives Milly one last desperate look, just before he disappears inside.

'And guess what?' continues Milly. 'At Swindel, every day starts with an exam. Even the first day of term. If you fail, you get an extra exam the next day. Some kids end up with all exams and nothing else.'

'Why don't their parents complain?'

'Complain?' she snorts. 'The parents *love* Swindel, cos of the exam results. They're some of the best in the country.'

'But don't they care that their kids hate it?'

'They just tell their kids that school isn't meant to be fun. They say that the point of school is to turn you into a winner.'

'A winner at what?'

'No idea.'

'Hey you two!' demands a harsh voice. 'What are you gawping at?' It's the whistle-blowing teacher: he's spotted us staring through the railings. We sprint back into the Clods crowd, right to the middle.

'So I guess we're lucky to be at Clods?' I ask Milly.

'Yes and no,' she replies knowingly.

'What d'you mean?'

'Well, they say that it's nice and friendly. That's the good bit.'

'What's the not-so-good bit?'

She's just about to answer, when – R–ing! Ri–! R–! – Clods' bell creaks into life again. She grabs my arm and leads me indoors. 'Time for our first lesson. You'll soon see for yourself!'

CHAPTER 13

Mr Kulla

'Morning, Year Sevens! And welcome to the wonders of science!'

It's my first Clods lesson. I'm with Milly and the rest of the class, huddled around Mr Kulla's table. We're wearing goggles because he's about to show us an experiment.

Only one person isn't paying attention: the glossy-haired girl who called me Frizz-Face. She's standing at the back, taking loads of selfies to show off her 'science goggle' look.

Milly nudges me back to attention. 'Ignore her, Kayla. She's not worth it.' I open my notebook and write: 'Kayla Grub, Clods College, Senior Science Lesson #1.'

I'm impressed by Mr Kulla because he seems like a top scientist. He's as bald as an egg, but with fuzzy hair sticking out on each side. His large forehead is propping up three pairs of glasses. He's even got the white coat and spotty bow tie. If you went to a fancy-dress party as a scientist, you'd copy Mr Kulla's look, down to the plastic gloves he's now putting on.

'Observe closely,' he begins, pouring some slurpy green stuff into a glass funnel. The funnel's attached to a line of glass tubes – and beneath the final tube, a little flame is flickering away. As the green goo oozes along each tube, we scribble away in our notebooks, feeling clever and scientific.

'Now you probably think that this substance is just any old green goo,' he announces.

'Yes I do, actually,' whispers Milly, winking at me.

'But you'd be wrong!' he continues, fiddling with a dial. 'Watch what happens when I gently turn up the heat. The trick is to do it ever so slightly.'

The flame suddenly roars away like it's powering a rocket. The goo starts to bubble, slowly at first but then faster and faster, making the tubes rattle. Green steam spurts out at the top.

'Hmm...' frowns Mr Kulla. 'Perhaps the heat is excessive.' But when he goes to turn down the dial, it comes off in his hand. 'Ah,' he says, scratching his head. 'Temporary setback.'

No one's making notes any more. We're standing with open mouths, not knowing whether to help Mr Kulla, or run for cover.

'Let's stand back a bit,' murmurs Milly. 'I've got a feeling this isn't gonna end well.'

'What d'you mean?' I whisper. 'Mr Kulla knows what he's doing. That's why he wears a white coat.'

She still pulls me away from the table, and we're only just in time. BANG! The green goo explodes, shattering the glass funnels and tubes. It shoots upwards like an erupting volcano, splatting against the ceiling. A few blobs of goo land on the kids standing at the front, but it's Mr Kulla who takes the full force of the impact.

'Don't worry!' he calls out. 'It's not as hot as it looks. In fact it's pleasantly warm. Just a little sticky.' A final goo-blob lands on the flame, putting it out.

For some reason, Mr Kulla doesn't seem surprised. 'Shame,' he sighs, wiping his goggles clean. 'Somehow that happens every time. Perhaps I keep getting the mixture wrong? Or the temperature? Science is a bit tricky like that, isn't it? One day I'll get the hang of it.'

'In your dreams,' snorts the glossy-haired girl from the back of the class.

'I beg your pardon, young lady?' he replies, taken aback.

She raises her voice to a shout. 'Call yourself a scientist? What a load of old goo!'

Some of the kids laugh nervously.

'Name, please!' he demands.

'Trixie Minx,' she replies defiantly.

'Well Miss Trixie Minx, let's see what Miss Skipper has to say about your cheekiness.'

'Go right ahead,' she smirks. 'When Scarecrow Skipper asks to see me, I'll tell her that the science bit of your brain is missing. Probably fell out in one of your explosions.'

Mr Kulla tenses with alarm. 'In that case, perhaps we'll... umm... let it go for now.'

The rest of the class can't believe it: Trixie's bullying him and he daren't stand up to her! We feel so sorry for him, we help him to clear up the mess.

'Oh dear,' I whisper to Milly. 'Mr Kulla isn't a brilliant scientist, after all.'

'Nope.'

'Not even average.'

'Uh-huh.'

'In fact, he's absolutely hopeless.'

'You got it.'

Mr Kulla himself is still pretty upbeat. 'Next week, we'll repeat the Great Goo Experiment!' he announces cheerfully. 'Homework: decide which goo colour we should try next time round. Let your imagination run wild! Need inspiration? It's right above you.'

We look up at the ceiling, which is covered in crazy wild splashes, in every shade you can think of. I start counting them, trying to work out how many Great Goo Experiments Mr Kulla has tried before.

'Pretty, isn't it?' he enthuses. 'Our very own art gallery! In fact I take the spare goo home with me, to use in my paintings. It's taking my art to a new level.'

'You like painting, Sir?' asks a tall kid called Martin.

'Doesn't everyone, Martin? Art is the best thing in the world!' He reaches inside his desk drawer and pulls out some of his paintings to show us. 'Behold a few of my humble attempts.'

Most of us gasp with admiration. 'Wow, Sir! They're amazing!' Mr Kulla has turned his leftover goo into mini masterpieces. He's even created a goo version of the Mona Lisa.

We head to the mid-morning break, full of chatter about this new twist.

'Mr Kulla's a genius!' Milly tells me. 'A true artist!'

'But how does that help us, Mills? He's here to teach us science, and he's the worst science teacher in the world.'

'It's not just Mr Kulla,' she replies. 'The other teachers are just as bad. None of 'em can teach what they're meant to.'

'How d'you know?'

'Oh, I can't help hearing the gossip.'

I'm still trying to get my head round this, when the Clods bell croaks back to life and we have to rush to our next lesson.

CHAPTER 14
Miss Zinc

'Morning, Year Sevens! Welcome to your artistic journey of discovery, here at Clods. Painting, drawing, printing, sculpture: what riches for us to explore together!'

Our art teacher, Miss Zinc, looks very creative. She's wearing a floaty patterned dress and chunky jewellery that jangles when she moves. As she strides to the front of the classroom, she twists her hair into a knot and sticks some artists' brushes through it to hold it together. 'Nice touch,' whispers Milly.

I'm impressed too, and can't wait to begin. The paint smudge on Miss Zinc's forehead makes me even more certain that she's the right person for the job.

Clutching a fistful of marker pens, she gathers us around her drawing board and explains our first task. 'Let's start with a little exercise that unlocks the inner artist. We'll take it in turns to draw something, and the others will guess what it is. Don't worry, I'll go first. You'll soon get the hang of it!'

She launches in, energetically covering the page in wild red streaks. She adds blue splats then finishes it off with black blobs, purple loops and yellow zig-zags. Slightly out of breath, she turns to us in triumph. 'OK folks, what have I drawn? I know the answer's obvious, but can someone please say it?'

There's an awkward silence. Her drawing looks like it was done by a drunk person with their eyes shut. What's it meant to show? We haven't a clue.

Milly pipes up. 'We're lost for words, Miss.'

'Thank you,' smiles Miss Zinc. 'I'm flattered.' But as the silence drags on, she gets impatient. 'Come along, class. Don't be shy. Speak up!'

'Giraffe?' asks a kid called Leon. She thinks he's joking. 'Ha ha! Very funny, Leon! Now can someone please give the proper answer?'

We all shout out different guesses:

'Teapot?'

'Pizza?'

'Toilet roll?'

I say 'hairbrush?'

Milly says 'baby dragon that's being sick?'

'No, no, no!' replies Miss Zinc, annoyed now. 'I have of course drawn the night sky, showing the movement of the stars, together with a cluster of asteroids, meteors and black holes.'

We're all stunned. You'd never guess that – not in a million years. 'Why wasn't it obvious?' she demands. 'Why does this happen every time?'

'I'll tell you why,' shouts Trixie. 'Because you can't draw, Miss Zero-Zinc! You're worse than rubbish. I've seen better efforts from babies.'

'Name?' barks Miss Zinc, dipping a paintbrush into a pot, ready to write it down.

'Trixie Minx at your service. But I wouldn't report me to Scarecrow Skipper if I were you. Not unless you want me to tell her that we should swap you for a paint-throwing monkey.'

Miss Zinc trembles until her jewellery jangles. She knows that Trixie's got her cornered. She drops the paintbrush and leans against her drawing board for support.

'Shall we have a go at drawing now, Miss?' asks Leon, trying to lighten the mood. Miss Zinc nods bravely. 'Good idea, Leon. Let's continue.'

We all take it in turns to do a drawing, and this time it's easy because we're much better artists than Miss Zinc.

Milly draws a mermaid and everyone guesses it before she's even added the shell necklace. I draw a flamingo and only Leon guesses something different. But I don't mind, because he says 'pelican' - which is almost the same thing.

But here's the crazy thing: when Miss Zinc comments on our drawings, she always comes at it from a science angle. She describes how Milly's mermaid would breathe through her gills to get oxygen into her blood. She explains that my flamingo's feathers are pink because of what it eats. When Leon draws Darth Vader, she reveals how lightsabers might actually work.

'That's amazing, Miss!' says Milly. 'How come you're such a science whizz?'

'Oh, it comes naturally,' smiles Miss Zinc. 'I study science whenever I get a spare moment. It's the best subject in the world!'

We're out of time, so she quickly announces our homework: 'Think about how apple trees are designed to scatter their seeds. Hint: it's something to do with the pips.'

I put my hand up. 'Isn't that science again, Miss? What about the art bit?'

'Good point, Kayla. Please draw an apple too. Then we've covered both!'

Weird. In my first morning at Clods, I've met a science teacher who's better at art, and an art teacher who's better at science. It doesn't make sense. It's all mixed up. And one of my classmates is scary and dangerous: Trixie Minx can say what she likes and get away with it.

I want to ask Milly about these big puzzles, but we're too busy getting lunch and finding our next classroom. I just hope that this afternoon's teachers can teach what they're meant to.

CHAPTER 15

Mr Prior

'Afternoon, Year Sevens! Welcome to the cutting-edge of computer science, here at Clods. Together, we'll explore digital technology and see how it's shaping our lives. We'll sharpen our own computing skills. We'll peer into the future by trying out some of the latest techno gadgets. I can't wait to begin!'

I take a good look at Mr Prior's flashy kit. The super-slim smartphone poking out of his pocket. The tiny microphone pinned to his shirt. The virtual reality headset perched on top of his head. His sleek desk, piled with copies of *Computer Nerd Weekly*. He looks impressive, but can he actually live up to it? Or will he be a disaster, like our two teachers this morning?

'OK folks,' he begins. 'I'll start by giving you a quick tour of my own laptop. It's got some pretty cool features that aren't widely available yet.' But he can't remember how to switch it on. He turns it round and round, looking for the Start button.

Some of the kids are already looking at Trixie, waiting for her to say something shocking. She whisks out her smartphone and whispers: 'You just wait. It'll be so worth it!'

A curly-haired girl called Bella steps in to help. 'The Start button's top right, Sir'. She plugs a cable into his laptop and now his screen projects onto the wall, so we can all see it.

'Oh dear,' says Mr Prior. 'Now it wants my password. I'm sure I wrote it down somewhere.' He pulls out some scraps of paper from his pockets, but they turn out to be shopping lists.

We all step in, trying to jog his memory.

'Maybe your password is your birthday, Sir?'

'Or your mum's name?'

'Or your favourite food?'

'Or the pet you had when you were little?'

He tries each suggestion, but none of them work.

In the end, Bella helps him to set up a new password and his laptop finally kicks into life. 'Eureka!' he shouts, looking pleased with himself. But now his screen is frozen.

'You need to accept the cookies,' Bella tells him.

'Accept the what-ies?'

'The cookies.'

'Excuse me, young lady: this is computer science, not cookery!'

'Plus you need to plug in your mouse,' she continues, patiently.

'Mouse?' he shrieks. 'Where?' He jumps up onto his chair, terrified. Bella accepts the cookies for him, and his laptop pings with an email.

'Let's take a look, shall we?' he says, bending down from his chair and clicking Open.

> *To: prior@clods.ac.uk*
>
> *From: TrixieTheMinx@me.com*
>
> *Re: Suggestion*

My pet goldfish knows more about computers than you do. Shall I ask it to teach next week's lesson? Or shall I simply tell Scarecrow Skipper that you're a waste of teacher space?

Mr Prior breaks out in a sweat, trying to delete the message. His virtual reality headset falls off his head, thudding onto the keyboard. The screen says *Spam Alert!*, sends out a shower of sparks, and dies.

He seems almost relieved. 'That's all for today, folks!'
'But we've still got half an hour left,' points out Bella.
'In that case, let's think some more about the mouse.'
'Good idea, Sir!' says Bella. 'We could start with its electronic signals?'
'Actually, I was thinking of the small, furry kind. This mouse has played such a big part in human history!'

He climbs down from his chair and paces around, telling us how mice used to sneak onto sailing ships, hidden in sacks of grain. Which leads him onto the history of sea travel. Which leads him onto the history of maps. Which leads him onto the history of printing.

Everyone except Trixie listens to him, spellbound. He may be a rubbish computer scientist, but he knows loads about history, and now we're actually learning something.

'How come you know all this stuff, Sir?' asks Milly.
'Oh, I just read lots of history books. And watch history programs. And attend history conferences. History is the best subject in the world!'
'But how d'you remember all the dates, Sir?'
'The trick is to get into the story, then the dates just fall into place. Which brings us to homework: let's

have another think about the mouse. Write something about its history. Including some dates.'

'Which mouse, Sir? Animal or computer?'

'Animal, of course. It's just... so... historical!'

'But Sir, aren't we meant to be doing computers?'

He wafts away the objection. 'Just try to write it on a computer, then that's the tech side covered. Good luck, everyone! More mouse history next week – excellent!'

When the bell goes, I stumble out of the classroom in a daze. Sure, the history's great - but will it even count? And how will we ever learn about computer science? Will Clods ever help me pass a single exam? There's one more lesson left today but I'm already losing hope.

As Milly and I head to the next classroom, I go really quiet. She asks me what's up, but I can't put it into words. I just have the sinking feeling that our next teacher will turn out to be another disaster, and that Trixie Minx won't miss the chance to stir up trouble.

CHAPTER 16

Mrs Hacker

History. Our final lesson of the day.

Our teacher, Mrs Hacker, is dressed to bring different periods of history to life – all in one outfit. She's wearing dungarees and a headscarf, like those engineer women from the Second World War. She's added a Celtic brooch, a 1970s hippy headband, and a Tudor lacy collar. Her shoes are historical, too: a Roman sandal on one foot and a wooden clog on the other. She's even tied an old-fashioned quill feather to her biro, so it wiggles around when she writes.

'What a mess!' smirks Trixie to her followers. 'Why doesn't she just pick one century and stick to it?' They titter, and jostle with each other to sit next to her.

'Afternoon, Year Sevens!' begins Mrs Hacker. 'Together we're going to explore the past, and see how it's shaped the life we know today. In other words, a journey through time itself! Let's start with a little slideshow to set the scene.'

She flicks a switch on her laptop. It dims the lights and projects a picture of Queen Elizabeth the first onto the wall behind her. 'One of our key historical figures!' she announces grandly. 'We even know her favourite hobby!' Then she goes blank. 'That hobby was...errr...'

'Video games!' prompts Trixie.

'Gosh, really?' replies Mrs Hacker gratefully. 'What's your name, young lady? You seem to be rather an expert.'

'Trixie Minx. And I love history, cos it's full of battles and torture and murder!'

A helpful girl called Yasmin isn't convinced. 'But Mrs Hacker,' she frowns. 'Surely video games weren't invented all that time ago?'

'Ah yes, good point. This queen's hobby was of course football. She was a World Cup super-fan. And she loved a good kick-around, despite the long dress and heavy crown.'

'But football wasn't invented then, either!' protests Yasmin.

'Ah yes, silly me. Now, what was she into? Of course! The Eurovision Song Contest! That's it.'

'But *all* of these things came along much later!' insists Yasmin.

'Really?' asks Mrs Hacker. 'No football? No Eurovision Song Contest? Poor Queen Victoria!'

'It's Queen Elizabeth the first, you dimwit!' hisses Trixie, but Mrs Hacker doesn't hear. She ploughs on with her slideshow, jumbling the whole of history into a hopeless mish-mash. She tells us that:

* King Henry the eighth was addicted to Facebook.
* William Shakespeare wrote episodes of *EastEnders*.
* The Second World War was fought with bows and arrows.

Trixie decides it's time to attack. 'Hey Miss, now I know why your clothes are so mixed up. You can't tell one end of a century from another!'

'How dare you!' splutters Mrs Hacker. 'You'll stay behind this afternoon and write a ten-page essay on Shakespeare's *EastEnders* scripts.'

'I don't think so,' smirks Trixie. 'Unless you want me to tell Scarecrow Skipper that the only date you can remember is your own birthday?'

Mrs Hacker realises that she's no match for Trixie. She smooths down her lacy collar and turns to the rest of the class. 'For those who still wish to learn history, let's end with a little animation that I put together.' She presses a button on her laptop and up pops a film.

We watch wide-eyed with admiration, because it shows Shakespeare and Queen Victoria, singing and dancing together in the Clods canteen! Shakespeare does a nifty tap-dance on the serving table, while Queen Victoria cartwheels around him, before diving into a giant bowl of custard. Even Trixie's impressed, though she tries not to show it.

'Wow Miss!' gasps Yasmin. 'Did you really make that film yourself?' 'Sure,' shrugs Mrs Hacker. 'It was easy. I just had to merge a couple of apps, then write a bit of computer code to fill in the gaps.'

'Can you really build computer programs?' asks Milly.

'Sure,' she shrugs again. 'Can't everyone? Computer science is the best subject in the world! But for this class, I'm afraid we're meant to stick to history. So please come along next week wearing something historical. I'm sure we'll find something to talk about.'

Great. So Mrs Hacker's a computer whizz. But she's still the worst teacher in history, and Trixie won't let her forget it.

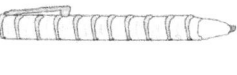

CHAPTER 17

Home Time

As I walk to the school gate with Milly, I can't stop thinking about our crazy weird teachers:
* Our science teacher is better at art.
* Our art teacher is better at science.
* Our computer teacher is better at history.
* Our history teacher is better at computers.

It doesn't make any sense. But if Granny were here now, she'd tell me to stay positive. So I put on a bright smile and stride out confidently. 'Maybe it's not so bad, Mills. Yes, we're gonna fail at science and art and history and computer technology. But at least the other teachers can't be any worse!' Somehow this doesn't sound as cheerful as I'd hoped.

'But Kayla,' she frowns. 'That's what I've been trying to tell you. Our other teachers are just as bad. Like I say, I've picked up a lot of gossip.'

I feel like the ground's falling away beneath my feet. 'Surely some of them are OK?' I plead. 'What about our music teacher?'

'Miss Wurdy? She sings like a frog with a sore throat. And her guitar's only got one string.'

'What about maths?'

'Mr Props? His sums always come out wrong, cos he muddles up his 6s and 9s.'

'Games, then?'

'Miss Hillock? If there's a ball, she'll trip over it.'
By the time Milly's finished, I've learnt that:
* Mr Champion (geography) thinks that Mount Everest is in Wales.
* Mr Platter (French) doesn't know the French for 'I'm a French teacher'.
* Mrs Parler (cookery) can't even boil an egg.

'But why?' I demand, stamping my foot. 'Why are they all so bad? Why doesn't anyone fix it?'

Milly shrugs. 'Dunno. We all just muddle along.'

'Why don't the parents make a fuss?'

'Because Clods is nice and friendly, Kayla. At least it was until Trixie came along. The parents are just glad that no one bunks off school. OK, the exam results aren't brilliant, but the top marks are always bagged by the Swindel kids anyway.'

I peer through the railings and watch those top-scoring Swindel kids head home. They're too worn out to chat to each other. Some of them have started their homework already: they're scribbling things down as they walk along.

A Swindel teacher comes out to shoo the last kids away. He blows his whistle so angrily, his cheeks swell into red balloons and his eyes are popping out of his head. He slams the school gates shut – CLANK – and stomps back inside.

I turn to watch the Clods kids swarming past us. They're laughing and joking. They're happy. Milly can see that I've got lots to think about.

'Nowhere's perfect,' she tells me. 'You'll soon get used to it. And Clods does have some good points.'

'Like what? Right now I can't think of anything!'

'Really?' she replies with a funny look. 'Hasn't Clods given you your very own loser to hang out with?'

'Hey Sis,' says a gloomy voice behind us. It's Milly's twin brother, Billy. Same height, same face, same chunky body. Same hair, but shorter. If they swapped school uniforms and wore wigs, I'd get them mixed up.

Milly puts her arm round him. 'Hey Bruv, meet Kayla. How's your first day at Swindel?' He gives me a shy smile. 'Hi Kayla. So you've ended up with my sister? Good luck, there!' She swipes at him with her schoolbag and he finally answers her question. 'Swindel? It was bad, bad, BAD.'

The three of us set off walking along the street. 'Bad in what way?' she asks him, gently.

'Oh, just everything!'

'Such as?'

He bursts out in a passion: 'Toxic teachers. Work overload. Exam deadlines. Even my banjo lesson was lousy. They locked me in a room until I could play twice as fast. They've turned my all-time favourite thing into a flippin' punishment!' He snaps a twig off a tree and uses it to thrash the bushes as we walk past.

'Maybe Mum might let you switch to Clods, after all?' suggests Milly, taking his banjo case off him so it doesn't get caught in the thrashing.

'Yeah, I'll just have to make her change her mind.'

'How?'

'Oh, I've got some ideas. It ain't gonna be pretty.'

I watch them head off together, and realise that today hasn't been so bad after all. Yes, the teachers are hopeless, but at least I'm not at Swindel. Plus I have a brand new bestie! Someone who doesn't care that I look and sound different. I set off home, feeling a big warm glow inside.

That glow turns to ice when Trixie appears and thumps me on the back. 'Still here, Frizz-Face? I see you've ended up with blubber-guts Milly Mobbs. Or should I call her *Gut-Bucket*? If she got any fatter, you could kick her around like a ball.' That stings me like a wasp, and I find myself yelling in her face: 'You lay off my bestie, or I'll –'

'You'll do what?' she smirks. 'Listen up, Frizz-Face: don't ever try to stand up to me. You'll regret it.' She whacks me on the back again and strides off.

I carry on home, trying to forget about Trixie and work out what I'll say to Mum and Dad. If they find out how bad my teachers are, they'll go mad with worry.

Can they complain to Miss Skipper? No: she's their boss and they can't afford to annoy her. Can they send me to another school? No: there's only Swindel and they've already shut me out. Can we move back to Olding? No: we need to stay here, for Granny.

I'll just have to pretend that my new teachers are brilliant. But will they believe me? When I was little, they could always tell when I was lying. Will it be any different now? My walk gets slower and slower. By the time I reach our front door, I'm dragging my feet along the pavement, scuffing the polish off my second-hand shoes. I pull out my key and let myself in.

61

CHAPTER 18

Home Alone

'Hi, I'm home!' I call up the stairs. 'Mum? Dad? Granny?' No reply. Just silence. Where are they? Shouldn't Mum and Dad be home from work by now? And where's Granny? She's too poorly to go anywhere. So why isn't she here?

The answer's on a note, pinned to the kitchen door. It's from Mum and I can tell she's in a hurry because it's a messy scribble:

Darling Kukoo, poor Granny's got worse so we're taking her to hospital. Try not to worry, sweetheart. Your tea's in the fridge – just pop it in the microwave. Dad and I will be back before your bedtime. PS. Can I suggest a spot of homework?

Oh no! What does 'got worse' mean? Granny was already poorly to start with. If she gets any weaker, she won't even be able to squeeze my hand anymore.

Maybe it's because I'm upset, but I suddenly feel hungry, even though it's nowhere near teatime. I open the fridge and gasp with surprise: Mum's made my all-time favourite meal!

* First, a fried-egg-and-cheddar sandwich.
* Second, a triple-choc pudding.
  (Choc sponge, choc sauce, choc sprinkles.)

This meal isn't very healthy (Mum says), so I'm only allowed it on special days like my birthday. But maybe today counts too, because of starting my new school.

'Any chance I can eat it right now?' I ask Cleo, who's winding in and out of my legs. She gives me a disappointed look that says 'Have you forgotten about Granny already? Shouldn't you stick to something more miserable? A plain cracker, perhaps? Followed by a sip of water?'

I remind her that Granny would want me to keep my strength up. So I scoff the lot, wiping my mouth on my sleeve and licking my fingers. Cleo's really cross with me now. She strides off with her tail in the air, leaving me to do the washing up.

I can't face that pile of dirty dishes just yet; I'll do anything to get out of it – even my homework. I shove my dirty dishes to one side, put my feet up on the coffee table (bliss!) and pull the books out of my schoolbag. OK, here we go.

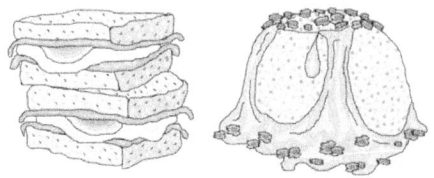

CHAPTER 19

Nice Work

First up, science from Mr Kulla: 'What shade of goo should we experiment with next week, and why?'

Easy! I don't even have to chew my pen before writing my answer: 'Let's go for bright yellow. Once it's splattered all over the ceiling, the room will look nice and sunny, even when it's raining. Because Art transforms things!'

Maybe he wanted more detail? But hey, I've used the word 'transform', and given 'art' a capital A. So that has to be worth something.

Next, Miss Zinc: 'How do apple trees scatter their seeds? Hint: pips. If you have time, draw an apple too.'

I have to chew my pen for this one, but I soon work it out: 'Birds and other animals think the pips taste great, so they don't spit them out. Then they go and poo all over the place, and the pips are in their poo, and that's the scattering sorted. It's science in action.'

I'm pleased with that last sentence. I bet it's the sort of thing those Swindel kids say, to get their top marks.

I still have time to draw an apple, so I go over to Granny's fruit bowl to pick one out. But it's empty apart from one banana, so I draw that instead. 'Sorry it's not an apple,' I write underneath. 'We don't have much time for shopping since Granny got ill.'

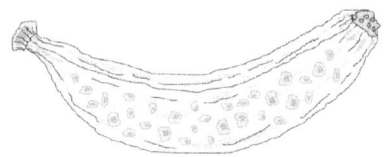

Now it's computer science from Mr Prior: 'Write some (animal) mouse history. Do it on a computer so it counts as computer homework.'

I go over to our family laptop and do a bit of research, before typing my mini-essay: 'Mickey Mouse was invented in 1928. In 1990, he finally met Kermit the Frog. Did Mickey feel that it was worth the wait? It's one of the great riddles of history.'

Another awesome last sentence. Plus I've used two TV characters! I'll mention this to Mum and Dad, next time they claim that TV isn't good for me.

Finally, Mrs Hacker: 'Find something historical and wear it to next week's class.' There's bound to be something in Granny's wardrobe. I scoot up to her room, to see what I can find.

CHAPTER 20

Granny's Room

I feel a bit guilty sneaking into Granny's room, especially as Cleo's spying on me from behind the curtain. 'You can drop the attitude,' I tell her. 'I'm doing proper homework. And anyway, who's around for me to ask?'

I start by taking Granny's clothes out of the wardrobe, carefully folding them into neat piles on the bed. Just when I thought the wardrobe was empty, something catches my eye in the bottom drawer. Oh wow, it's a beautiful old-fashioned necklace! A dainty chain, threaded through a golden key.

I pick it up and wipe off the dust. The key's stamped with a pattern that catches the light. It gleams and glimmers, like it's come back to life. I could look at it for hours.

Even more amazing is the label, tied at the end. Here, Granny's written two words that make me dance inside: 'For Kayla'!

If Granny wants me to have it, why hasn't she told me about it? And what does the key open? I can't wait to ask her. This necklace is nearly mine, after all.

It's also perfect for my next history class. Even Trixie will be jealous! With a delicious thrill, I put it round my neck and model it in front of Granny's mirror. For once, the girl staring back at me doesn't look too bad. Even her frizzy hair doesn't matter so much. She's an almost-twelve year old, ready to face the world.

I carefully wrap it in a tissue and put it in my pocket.

Now I just need to put everything back in the right place. But when I turn round to the bed, those neat piles of clothes have gone! They've turned into a sprawling mess, with a wriggling cat buried deep inside.

'Cleo!' I yell. 'Have you no shame?' She peeps out at me, a pair of Granny's knickers twisted around her head. I grab the knickers off her and give them a good shake. The cat hair flies off them and lands on the rest of the clothes. Damn! Cleo realises that she's messed up, and goes to sulk in the corner.

With superhuman patience, I untangle the clothes jumble, pick off the cat hairs, and put everything back where I found it. Granny's favourite cardigan is the last piece of the jigsaw, and when I go to brush the pocket clean, there's a brand new surprise.

Something falls out of the pocket. An envelope, labelled in Granny's writing:

For Kayla. For when I've gone.

Where is Granny planning to go? Surely she doesn't mean... dying? OK, I know that Granny's old, but she's not allowed to go and die. Not for years and years yet. Perhaps not ever. I won't let it happen. I need her too much.

I can feel the note inside, but I can't read it because the envelope's stuck down with sellotape. That's when I realise that Granny doesn't want me to know about it. With a thud of disappointment, I realise that this includes the necklace, too.

I try it on, one final time - loving how it makes me feel. If only Cleo hadn't jumped out of her corner to give a brand new lecture. 'Have you no shame, Kayla Grub? Put that necklace back, and pretend you never saw it!'

I can't ignore that warning, or the way she's attacking my ankle. I hide the necklace back in Granny's bottom drawer, and curse the day I asked for a cat.

What will I say when Mrs Hacker asks me to show what I've brought? I'll just have to pretend that I forgot. Everyone except Milly will laugh at me – and Trixie will laugh most of all.

Burning with resentment, I give the room a final tidy, switch off the lights, and plod back downstairs.

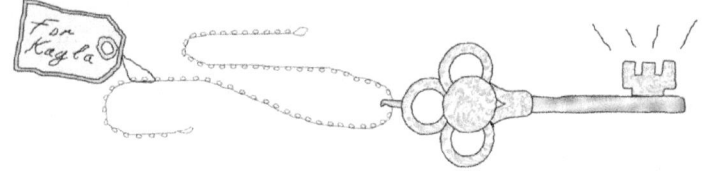

CHAPTER 21

Grown-Up Lying

I've still got the rest of the evening to myself, to watch as much TV as I want. But all I can think about is the secret note and necklace, hidden in Granny's wardrobe. And I can't even ask anyone about them. All I can do is switch off the TV, do the washing up, and wipe my footprints off the coffee table.

By the time Mum and Dad get home I'm already in my pyjamas, with my schoolbag packed for tomorrow.

The first thing they do is sweep me up into a hug that lifts my feet off the floor. But it's not a happy hug; it's because they're upset.

'Where's Granny?' I ask, wriggling free.

They blink back tears. 'She needs to stay in hospital. But the nurses have made her nice and comfy, and we'll go to see her every day.'

'When is she coming home?'

'Not for a while, Kukoo. But she sends her special love to you.'

I gulp hard to stop myself blubbing like a baby. I'm sure that Granny's worse than they're pretending. So why are they lying? Is it because they love me, and don't want me to worry? Does that make the lie OK?

Dad makes an effort to sound brighter. 'Come on then, Kukoo: how was your first day at Clods?'

I remind myself to stick to the positive, and tell them all about Milly. 'She sounds great,' they reply. 'But what about your education? Are you going to win lots more certificates and trophies? What are your lessons like? And your teachers?'

'My teachers?' I repeat, stupidly. I knew this question was coming. Now it's my turn to lie, and I can't afford to mess it up.

'Yes, Kukoo. Your teachers. What are they like?'

I mumble and stare at my feet. 'Actually it's kind of difficult to put it into words.' Why the hell didn't I prepare this properly? Now the moment's here, I'm really struggling.

They're determined to get an answer. 'Come on, Kukoo. We're dying to hear all about them!'

'Well if you must know, I guess that my teachers are very... sort of...'

'Yes?'

'SPECIAL!' Oh, is that really the best word I can come up with? No wonder I'm squirming like a worm on a hook. There again, I haven't said that my teachers are any good. Just 'special'. Which is true in a way. Maybe I'm getting the hang of grown-up lying, after all.

Before they can ask more questions, I change the subject. 'How was *your* first day at Clods? Are your new jobs OK?' My simple question brings a sparkle to their eyes and puffs out their chests with pride.

'My washing up was praised by the dinner ladies!'

'The Head Caretaker loved my ironed overalls!'

Well thank goodness for that. My new teachers may be rubbish, but at least Clods is going well for Mum and Dad. That makes it a success for two out of three Grubs, and I'll try to be at least two-thirds happy.

When I snuggle under my duvet, Cleo stays sulking under my chair, waiting for me to apologise. I've barely spoken to her, since I shouted at her for messing up Granny's clothes.

'Hey I'm sorry, Cleo,' I begin, reaching out to stroke her. 'You didn't mean to spoil anything. You were only trying to help.'

She edges towards me, but then waits for me to say something else. 'I know, Cleo, I know. I shouldn't look through Granny's stuff without asking.'

That's what she was waiting to hear. She leaps onto my bed and snuggles around my feet, purring away. It's as though we never fell out.

At least Cleo and I don't have to lie to each other; we got past that stage long ago. If only everyone else could be so simple.

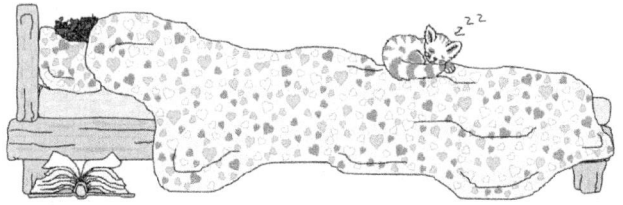

CHAPTER 22

Decision Time

It's day two of Clods - and before I do anything else, I need to put things right with Milly. I've realised that I messed up with her, too. I track her down in the playground, first thing. 'Hey Mills, I'm dead sorry about yesterday.'

'Huh?' she frowns.

'When I said that Clods is a disaster.'

'Still don't follow you?'

'I forgot about you being my brand new bestie. That's a good thing about Clods. A very good thing. So I'm sorry.'

'Hey that's OK, hun. No hard feelings.'

'Great. Cos I really am sorry.'

'Kayla, if you say *sorry* one more time, I'll go off and be besties with someone else!' She swings her schoolbag at me and we crease up laughing.

'How's Billy?' I ask, serious again. 'Is your mum gonna let him switch to Clods?'

'She said she'd rather starve in the gutter. Trust me, Kayla: that's never gonna happen. Even so, he's started a protest, to try and change her mind.'

'What kind of protest?'

'Last night, he found a tin of black paint in the garage and he slapped it all over his bedroom walls.

Now it looks like a cave. It's gross. Stinks, too. But Mum's just ignoring him.'

'So what happens now?'

'He's planning to do something even worse.'

'Like what?'

'He won't say, Kayla. That's what freaks me out. What if he jumps off a cliff? Or rides his bike into the canal? Or buries himself in a graveyard? Or –'

'No way! Why would he deliberately hurt himself?'

'Cos he's desperate!' she wails. 'I've never seen him so trapped, and he's only been at Swindel for one day!'

Now I'm worried about him, too. But for the rest of the week, he doesn't go mental. He just covers his room in a fresh layer of black paint, to top up the smell.

And what about Clods? Well, Trixie's still gunning for Milly and me, but it only hurts us a bit, because we're besties for life. We sit together in every class, giggling every time our teachers mess up. Which is all the time. None of them can teach what they're meant to, but they battle away, as if they've got no choice. School's one long comedy show, funnier than anything online. The work's easy too, because we're always one step ahead of the teachers.

By week two, though, I start to feel differently. My teachers don't seem funny anymore. Now I'm just bored, and stare out of the window.

Even so, I'm glad I've lied to my parents about it. It's a big secret to carry all by myself, but I reckon I'm doing the right thing. They've already got loads to worry about, because Granny's still in hospital. At least they think I'm getting a good education. 'Thank goodness we all ended up at Clods,' they say, with a sigh of relief.

Week two brings new problems for Milly too, because Billy's stepped up his protest. He's used a pin to scratch a message on his arm: SWINDEL SUCKS. He shows us one day after school, pulling up his shirt sleeve to reveal each scabby letter. 'Ouch!' I wince. 'That looks agony!'

'That's the whole point,' he replies grimly. 'I made sure that Mum saw the blood on my shirt. And when she's around, I keep my sleeves rolled up, so the message is loud and clear.'

'But will it change her mind? Will she switch you to Clods?'

'Fat chance. She's ignoring me.'

'What if the Swindel teachers see it?'

'At school, I cover it up with a bandage. The teachers think I'm injured. I've told 'em it's their fault, for making me do too much banjo practice.'

Milly stamps her foot. 'I can't bear to think of you hurting yourself! Will you please stop this stupid protest, before you do any more damage?'

'It's not stupid, Sis; it's my only hope. Swindel's destroying my soul. If you were me, you'd do the same.'

By week three, I've had my twelfth birthday, which makes me even keener to learn grown-up stuff. I want to know about poems and rain-clouds and jazz and... well... everything. Otherwise how can I understand the world? Or figure out what I can really do? At Clods, it's a non-starter.

It's Tuesday morning, and we're in double maths with Mr Props. As usual he's mixed up his 6s and 9s, making his sum collapse in a muddle. I'm scribbling in my notebook but it's not maths; it's a series of doodles:

Doctor Kayla, saving a patient's life.

Engineer Kayla, building a mega bridge.

Prime Minister Kayla, leading the country.

Astronaut Kayla, landing on Mars.

Will I ever get to do any of these things? Not if I stay at Clods. Not a chance. I close my notebook with a sigh.

'What's up?' whispers Milly.

'Do any of the Clods kids end up doing great things?'

'How d'you mean?'

'Well, do they ever become doctors or engineers? Or Prime Ministers? Or astronauts?'

'What a funny question! It's the Swindel kids who end up doing that sort of thing. Not us.'

I reopen my notebook and make another list:

Good things about Clods:

1. Not nasty Swindel.

2. Best friend Milly.

3. Mum and Dad jobs.

Bad things about Clods:

1. Rubbish teachers.

2. No future.

3. Not funny anymore.

I can't stand it any longer. Surely someone can explain why the teachers are so rubbish? Of course: Miss Skipper! I've never spoken to her before, but I'll go and see her this lunchtime, before I change my mind.

R–ing! Ri–! R–! As soon as the lunchtime bell goes, I head for Miss Skipper's office.

'Hey!' Milly calls out after me. 'Where are you off to?'
'Can't tell you. Sorry.'
'Mean! Can I come too?'
"Fraid not.'
'Extra-mean! You realise you'll miss lunch?'
'Yeah, I know. Don't suppose you could save me some chips?'
'Hmmff!' she snorts. 'Now you're having a laugh.'

I wish I could tell her what I'm up to, but asking Miss Skipper about the teachers is a really big deal. Something tells me I should keep it to myself, for now. With a final *sorry*, I turn my back on Milly and walk away. It feels horrible, but now that I've started I have to see it through.

Things get even worse when I reach Miss Skipper's door. Someone leaps up from behind and digs me in the ribs. I realise it's Trixie, before I even turn to face her. 'So you've been sent to the Scarecrow?' she smirks. 'Finally in trouble, Frizz-Face?'

I put on my best sarcastic voice: 'Ooh, wouldn't you love to know?'

'Whatever,' she shrugs, walking off. 'As if I care about your stupid little life, anyway.'

Wow! I stood up to Trixie and it sort of worked!

Miss Skipper's door is slightly open, so I count to three and knock firmly. A woman's voice says 'Come in'. No going back now. I step inside and close the door behind me.

76

CHAPTER 23

Miss Skipper

Miss Skipper's office is as old and scruffy as Miss Skipper herself. Every surface is piled high with books and papers. They're leaning in every direction, like they're about to topple over and bury her. But on her desk, there's a vase of yellow roses that makes the room bright and cheerful, despite all the mess.

She's reading an official-looking letter and it can't be good news, because she's clutching it in panic. I give a little cough and she glances at me, making an effort to smile. 'Kayla Grub, isn't it? New girl? How are you settling in at Clods?'

I take a deep breath, ready for my Big Speech about the terrible teachers. But just as I'm about to launch in, I hear someone creep up to the other side of the door. What if it's Trixie? Without stopping to ask Miss Skipper, I pounce to the door and fling it open.

Trixie's crouched down, trying to peep through the keyhole. She scrambles to her feet but it's too late: Miss Skipper sees her and explodes with fury. 'Trixie Minx! How dare you spy on a private meeting?'

For the first time ever, I see Trixie blush with shame, and her dark, flashing eyes look scared. 'S-sorry, Miss,' she stammers. 'I– I've lost my earring and I thought it might be down here.'

'Nonsense, young lady!' fumes Miss Skipper. 'You're wearing both earrings right now – as you well know. And may I remind you that such flashy jewellery has no place in my school. Now get away with you!'

'Yes Miss. Sorry Miss.' Trixie trudges away, removing her earrings as she goes.

Miss Skipper turns back to me. 'Now then Kayla, how can I help?'

Once again, I get ready to launch into my 'terrible teacher' speech. But this time, my eyes wander to the letter that she's still clutching. The title's written in capital letters that jump at me, right across the room:

INSPECTOR SNOOP ARRIVES THIS FRIDAY. YOU'VE BEEN WARNED!

Before I can stop myself, I blurt out: 'Who's Inspector Snoop, Miss?'

I'm expecting her to give me a lecture on minding my own business. But she answers me in a daze. 'He's the Chief Inspector of Schools. He's visiting Clods to assess our teachers.'

No wonder she looks worried; she must know that our teachers are rubbish. I risk another question. 'But Miss, why does it say *you've been warned*?'

'If he doesn't like what he finds, I'm afraid we're in big trouble.'

'What sort of trouble, Miss?'

This time I really think I've gone too far, but she gives me a straight answer. 'He could close us down.'

Close us down? Did she really say that? Where would that leave me? Milly too? And Mum and Dad?

She finally snaps back to her usual self. 'Oh my goodness, did I really say all those things out loud? I really should've been more discreet. But it seems you caught me by surprise, and I'm too tired to make anything up. I'm a hopeless liar anyway.'

'But Miss, it says that he's coming this Friday. That's only three days away!'

'Yes thank you, Kayla. I'm well aware of that. Now what did you want to see me about?'

'Doesn't matter, Miss. Another time.'

Halfway to the door, I pause again. 'Actually Miss, there *is* one thing you can help me with.'

'Yes, Kayla?'

'Please can you not tell my parents about this Inspector Snoop guy? They're already worn out with visiting Granny in hospital. And they love this school: it's given them the best jobs of their life.'

She smiles weakly. 'Very well, Kayla. There's no reason for your parents to know. Not yet, anyway. In fact, why don't we keep this to ourselves for now? If we told anyone else, it would only cause panic and make things worse. Let's just see how things go on Friday and hope for the best.'

'Yes Miss. Of course, Miss.'

'Thank you, Kayla. I've decided to trust you, so please don't let me down. Remember: not a word!'

She goes back to staring at the letter, now dabbing her forehead with a crumpled tissue. I creep away, feeling even worse than when I went in. Now I have to keep even more secrets. And tell even more lies.

CHAPTER 24

Top Secret

Minutes later, I'm in the canteen with Milly. 'Chips?' she begins brightly, handing me a huge plateful that's swimming in ketchup.

'Aw, you saved some for me, after all.'

'Yeah, cos I'm too soft for my own good.'

I make a start on them, but she can tell something's wrong. 'Where did you go just now, Kayla? What happened? You look kinda scared.'

'Oh, it's nothing really.'

'Don't believe you. What's going on?'

'Sorry Mills. Can't say.'

'Thought we were besties?' she pouts. 'Shouldn't we share all our secrets?'

'Yeah. But not this one.'

'Why?'

'Cos it belongs to someone else.'

'Who?'

'Can't say.'

We're going round in circles and she loses patience. 'Fine! If that's how you wanna play it – see you later.' She stomps off to sit with Yasmin and Bella, leaving me to finish my chips alone.

I might have guessed that Trixie would turn up to rub my nose in it. 'Lost your porky pal, Frizz-Face?'

She plonks down next to me and helps herself to my chips. 'Ooh, just how I like 'em!'

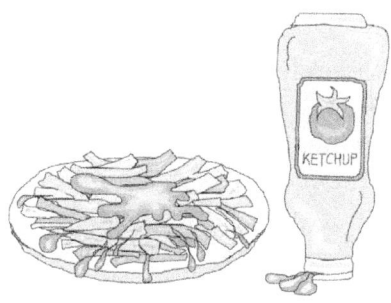

I try to grab my plate back, but she holds on tight. It's caught between us and the ketchup's spilling over our hands, like blood. She finally snatches it off me and walks off with it, cramming my chips into her mouth.

I try to drink some water, but my hands have gone shaky and it dribbles down my chin. So much for using this lunchtime to put everything right. It's been a total wipe-out.

That afternoon, Milly and I still sit together in class but we don't feel like friends anymore. We just say things like 'You need to return that pencil I lent you,' and 'I'd like my ruler back, now'. It's horrible.

And all this time, I'm carrying a terrible secret. Inspector Snoop's going to give my teachers a massive FAIL. Clods will shut down, which means no more school for me, and no more jobs for Mum and Dad. It'll be one big meltdown, starting this Friday.

I can't do anything to stop it. I can't even tell anyone about it – not even my bestie – because I promised not to.

Hang on, maybe there *is* someone I can talk to, without letting Miss Skipper down? Someone who's not part of Clods and won't tell the secret? Someone who listens to my problems without bossing me around or giving a lecture? Someone who treats me like a grown-up? Granny, of course.

I'll go and see her, straight after school.

CHAPTER 25

Hospital Visit

R–ing! Ri–! R–! Before the end-of-school bell has finished, I'm racing across the playground, heading for Granny's hospital. I know exactly where to go, because I've already visited her loads of times. Mum and Dad won't be there for ages, so I'll have her all to myself.

When I whizz past the hospital shop, I remember that I've still got today's lunch money. Hey, I'll spend it on a great big chocolate bar for Granny! Even better: one of them's 50% Extra Free! It's as heavy as one of those Swindel textbooks. I carry it to her ward like a trophy, so everyone can see it and get jealous.

You'd think that by now I'd be used to seeing how poorly she is. But when I reach her bed, I still get a shock. She looks even thinner and smaller than yesterday. She's propped up on pillows, because she's too weak to sit up.

At the top of her bed, there's a creepy machine that keeps beeping and flashing. Its tubes run all the way into her arms, as if she was part of the machine. There's even a little tube wrapped around her face, blowing air into her nose.

My Get Well Soon card is sitting right next to her bed. So why isn't it working? Why isn't she getting better? With a shudder, I remember Granny's secret note: *For Kayla. For when I've gone.* Well whatever that note says, I won't let her go anywhere. I'll make her stay around forever.

'Hi Granny,' I begin, trying not to stare at the beeping machines and scary tubes. I'm not allowed to hug her because of all the medical kit attached to her body. But there's a little patch on her cheek, in-between the tubes, where I can kiss her without anyone telling me off. So that's what I do.

'Darling Kayla,' she murmurs, squeezing my hand.

'Here you go, Granny. This'll pick you up in no time.' I hand over the chocolate with a flourish, pleased it's so big and chunky.

'How kind of you, sweetheart. But you know what I'd love most of all? To watch *you* enjoy it!'

Now I realise that she's too ill to eat it. Why am I such an idiot? She waits for me to tuck in, but I can't face it. I put it back in my bag and chew my lip instead.

'Kayla not eating chocolate? Tell me what's the matter, love. I've got all the time in the world. As you can see, I'm not going anywhere.'

'Oh Granny,' I blurt out. 'It's all gone wrong. Already!'

I tell her about the meltdown. My terrible teachers. The visit from Snoop. Clods shutting down, leaving me without a school, and Mum and Dad without a job. My bestie dumping me because I can't tell her this new secret. Watching her brother hurt himself because he's so unhappy. And on top of everything, being bullied by the prettiest girl in my class.

Granny's great. She doesn't tell me to grow up and get a grip. She's one in a million.

'You poor love,' she begins. 'So many problems, all at once! But maybe the teachers are one thing you can fix?'

'Really, Granny?' I'm so desperate to hear more, I clutch the sheets on her bed. To my horror, this pulls at her tubes and she winces with pain.

'Oh Granny, I'm so sorry. I'm a total moron. But can you think of a way to fix the teachers? Please please tell me!'

CHAPTER 26

Granny's Story

Granny closes her eyes. At first I think she's working out her answer, but she's simply fallen asleep. So I sit quietly, but it's hard to be patient when you're waiting for someone to wake up and sort out your life.

After the longest few minutes in history, she opens her eyes and picks up where she left off. 'So, your teachers need to impress the Inspector this Friday. Can't you find a way to help them?'

'You mean turn them from rubbish into brilliant?'

'From rubbish into impressive. Not always the same thing.'

'But Granny, Snoop's visiting in just three days' time. Plus I promised Miss Skipper that I wouldn't say anything to anyone. So you see: I'm stuck!'

She nods thoughtfully, and begins a story. 'Once upon a time, when Kayla was little, there was a special birthday present that she wanted Granny to buy for her. Her parents told Kayla to wait and see what Granny chose, but Kayla wanted to point Granny in the right direction. Can you remember what she did?'

'Of course!' I laugh. 'How could I forget?'

With twinkly eyes, she continues: 'Kayla wrote a note and hid it in Granny's handbag. In this note, Kayla explained which present she wanted, and asked

Granny to keep the note secret. Granny found the note and bought the present. And to this day, Kayla's parents think that the present was just a nice surprise!'

'It's a sweet story, Granny. But what's it got to do with my teacher problem?'

'All the clues are there,' she smiles. 'You'll work it out. I know you will!'

'But –'

'Time to go, young lady,' announces a nurse, bustling up to the bed.

'But –'

The nurse is firm. 'Come along now, please. Mrs Grub needs to rest.'

I kiss Granny's little patch of cheek again, then turn and wave just before I leave the ward. She can't wave back because of the tubes attached to her arms. But she winks at me, just like she used to, and I tell myself that she'll soon be coming home.

I need to head home too, but I can't afford the bus fare because I've spent all my money on that stupid chocolate. I set off walking instead, and with every step I think about Granny's story. What's she trying to tell me? Why can't I work it out?

As I put my key into our front door, the whole point of the story finally hits me, and a daring new plan springs into my head. Oh Granny, you clever thing! Maybe your idea really *can* fix the teachers! All I need to do is make it happen.

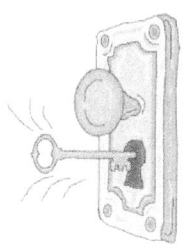

CHAPTER 27

Good Plan

I'm getting ready for school and working out my new plan. That's a lot of things going on at once. I think it's called *multi-tasking*.

Stage one is to tell the big secret to Milly. Yes, I know I promised Miss Skipper that I wouldn't tell anyone, but that's before I decided to try and save the school.

Cleo's already guessed what I'm up to, because she's giving me lots of hard stares – even now, when I'm on the toilet. 'Traitor!' those fierce eyes say. 'Promise-breaker! Sneaky tell-tale!'

It's hard to be dignified when your knickers are round your ankles, but I do my best. 'Listen, Cleo: your cat world may be simple, but my life's more complicated. I can't save Clods all by myself. With Milly's help, I've got half a chance.' Cleo's not convinced; she hisses a final warning and scampers off.

I go to find Milly as soon as I reach school. It's awkward at first, because after yesterday's fall-out, we're not exactly friends. But everything changes once I tell her about Snoop's visit. She starts by grabbing my arm, just like she used to. 'Blimey, Kayla. That's a biggie. No wonder you couldn't tell me, before.'

'No worries. Chocolate?' I open the bar that I bought for Granny, and we chomp away thoughtfully. Despite our new worries, it feels good to be friends again.

'But Mills, you mustn't tell anyone. Promise?'
'Only if you let me have that last chunk.'
'Deal.'

I want to tell her about my big new idea, but she's busy thinking up plans of her own. 'Hey Kayla, why don't we just pay this Snoop guy to leave us alone?'

'I can't afford it. I'm broke.'

'Yeah, but I'm loaded. I've still got £100 from my summer holiday. I was gonna spend it on pony treats, but I can hand it to Poop-Snoop, instead.'

'That's an amazing offer, Mills. But what if it's still not enough?'

'OK then. Let's bring school to a standstill.'

'How?'

'Doh! Set off the fire alarm.'

'Look, I'm not sure what films you've been watching, but that kind of thing never works in real life.'

'Hmmff. So what's *your* big idea, Miss Know-It-All?'

'Well since you ask, I reckon we could... sort of... teach the teachers!'

'Teach the teachers? Are you mad?'

She's right. I must be mad to suggest such a crazy idea, even though it's based on Granny's story from yesterday. But Milly's ideas are even worse. We've only got two days left and we have to do something.

'It's based on secret notes,' I begin, lamely.

'What kind of notes?'

'We write a note to each teacher, giving 'em lots of tips for their lessons. So they'll be more like proper teachers when Snoop turns up.'

'Why the hell would they take tips from *us*? In their eyes, we're just kids.'

'We pretend the notes are from Miss Skipper.'

'How? We don't even know her handwriting.'

'I saw it when I was in her office. It's big and messy.'

'But Kayla, we still have to hand the notes to the teachers. Please don't suggest we use a Miss Skipper disguise. We'd need a damn sight more than a crumpled suit!'

'No disguise needed. We simply slip the notes into the teachers' bags when they're not looking.'

'How do we stop 'em asking Miss Skipper about it?'

'The notes tell 'em not to discuss it with anyone.'

She pauses to think it over. Waiting for her decision is agony, but there's nothing more I can say. It doesn't get any easier when she declares a single word: 'Bonkers!'

'Me or the plan?'

'Both.'

'But it's all we've got. So will you help me, Mills?'

She breaks into a smile. 'Guess I have no choice.'

I'm so grateful, I don't know what to say.

'Hey, we can call it the TTTTT Plan!' she grins. 'That's our secret code for Teach The Truly Terrible Teachers! Nice, huh? When do we start?'

'Start what?' asks a sneering voice behind us. Trixie!

'Stay out of it, Manky-Minx,' snaps Milly. Trixie swipes Milly's bag off her shoulder, into a puddle. 'You won't keep your pathetic little secrets from *me*. I'm watching the pair of you, every step of the way.'

'Back off, Trixie,' I begin. 'Or else!'

'Or else what?' she scoffs. 'Ooh, I'm so scared!' Her dark eyes flash at me, defiantly.

Milly clenches her fists, ready to whack Trixie to the ground. Half of me wants to join in, but if we get into a fight now, those notes will never get written. I pick up Milly's bag and pull her away. Trixie calls out after us: 'You can run, but you can't hide. Whatever you're up to, I'll sniff it out!'

'Why does she hate us so much?' grumbles Milly as we march off.

'Wish I knew.'

'And how can we write those notes, without her sneaking up on us? Nowhere's safe.'

'Really? As far as I know, she's not allowed in my bedroom.'

'Ha ha! Good point. The perfect hiding place!'

'Can you come to my house today, after school?'

'No probs. The pony will just have to manage without me.'

'Can you bring an overnight bag, too?'

'Ooh, a sleepover! Even better!'

She doesn't realise that writing the notes is going to be hard work. But I don't want to make it sound too tough, in case she changes her mind.

R–ing! Ri–! R–! Time for another day of madness in the classroom. I wish we could start the notes right now, but we'll just have to wait until this evening.

CHAPTER 28

Mr Bunnyfun

Later that afternoon, Milly's on my doorstep. Her overnight bag's so big, she's had to drag it along the pavement. Something's poking out of the top. It looks like two fluffy ears.

'What on earth is that?' I ask. 'Is it alive?'

'Meet Mr Bunnyfun!' she giggles, unzipping her bag. It's a giant toy rabbit. Mr Bunnyfun slides out of Milly's bag and lands with a thud on the doorstep. He's the biggest stuffed toy I've ever seen.

She climbs over him and pulls him inside. 'Don't be too hard on me, Kayla. I know he's silly and childish. I know I'm too old for him. But he's here to bring us luck, see? I've had him since I was little, and he's never let me down.'

We try to drag him upstairs, but he's so big and heavy we get stuck halfway up. Then we can't move for laughing. A key turns in the front door. It's Mum and Dad, home from work. 'Hello?' Mum calls out. 'What's going on up there? Ah, you must be Milly. Nice to meet you.'

Milly's squashed beneath Mr Bunnyfun, but she cheerfully waves at Mum and Dad through a gap in the bannisters. 'Hello Mrs Grub. Hello Mr Grub. Nice to meet you too. Thanks for letting me stay.' That's the sort of reply that Mum and Dad call 'nice manners'. They're always going on at me about it.

'We'll leave you both to it,' grins Dad. 'You've obviously got your hands full.'

We haul Mr Bunnyfun up to my bedroom, and Milly stops to admire the door. 'Oh Kayla, it's gorgeous! And carved with your initials!' I can't help feeling proud, especially when I show off the little peephole.

When Milly's finished trying the peephole for herself, we squeeze Mr Bunnyfun inside and dump him onto my bed. He takes up half the room, but maybe he'll bring us luck, after all.

Cleo hates him, of course. She tries to push him away then stomps off in a huff. At least that leaves a bit more space for the rest of us. It's only a cat-sized bit of space, but we need every inch we can get.

Now that Mr Bunnyfun's settled, we line up our pens and paper on my desk, ready to write the teachers' notes. The sight of all those blank pages makes us go quiet. If we get the notes finished this evening, it'll be a miracle – even with Mr Bunnyfun cheering us on.

We go down to tea feeling a bit overwhelmed.

CHAPTER 29

Tea Time

Tea is plain pizza: just tomato sauce on top, and no fancy bits. It's the kind of thing we eat all the time because it's cheap. Or as Mum says: *good value*. I'm worried that Milly won't like it, but she wolfs down her first three slices and asks for more.

Then everything unravels. It starts when Mum says 'Another drink, Kukoo?'

'Kukoo?' echoes Milly, looking at me in wonder.

'Just a silly nickname,' I mumble, glaring at Mum and Dad.

'How come you never told me?' asks Milly. 'It's lovely. Can I call you Kukoo from now on?'

'No way! Or I'll tell the whole of Clods about Mr Bunnyfun!'

'But you call me Mills, not Milly.'

'That's different.'

'How?'

'Mills is a grown-up name.'

'Since when? Says who?'

Mum shoots us a warning glance. 'Now then girls, don't fall out.'

We're interrupted by a buzz on Milly's phone. 'What's up?' I ask, worried that our sleepover's cancelled.

'Nothing. Just a message from my mum.'

'What does she say?' asks Mum, who can't help being a bit nosey.

Milly reads it out loud: 'Don't you dare spend the whole evening watching trashy TV.'

'Well really!' explodes Mum, offended. 'This is not that sort of home. What does Mrs Mobbs think goes on here?'

Dad tries to calm her down: 'Please don't fuss, Krystal. I'm sure Mrs Mobbs doesn't mean it that way.'

'Actually, TV's off for tonight,' I explain. 'We'll be working on a homework project.'

'It's called the TTTTT Plan,' adds Milly, winking at me.

'Tee-tee-tee-tee-tee?' repeats Mum. 'Goodness! Whatever next?'

'What subject?' asks Dad.

Disaster! Milly and I answer at the same time, only she says *French* and I say *music*. We realise our mistake and make it even worse by swapping over: now she says *music* and I say *French*. There's a confused silence. In total desperation, I blurt out: 'It's musical French! Sorry, I mean French music!'

Milly splutters into her drink but Dad gives an impressed whistle. 'French music? Just the kind of thing to help people get on in life! If only I'd had the chance to study it when I was young. Maybe I'd be Head Caretaker by now, instead of just the Assistant.'

'Give it time, Kevin, give it time,' Mum tells him soothingly. 'Now you're at Clods, who knows where your talents will take you?' She turns back to Milly and me. 'Aren't you both lucky to have such brilliant teachers?'

I have to remind myself that Milly and I are lying to them for all the right reasons.

As soon as tea's finished and cleared away, Mum and Dad put on their coats. They're off to the hospital, to say goodnight to Granny. 'We'll be back by your bedtime,' Mum tells us. 'Good luck with the French magic.'

'French *music*,' says Dad, with another admiring glance at Milly and me.

This time, I manage to change the subject. 'Please could you give Granny a special message?'

'Sure, Kukoo. What is it?'

'Please could you tell her that I'm making good use of the story she told me.'

They look puzzled, but they're running late and haven't got time to ask. And maybe Mum's had enough of being nosey for one evening. 'OK Kukoo. We'll be sure to let her know.'

Milly and I run upstairs and shut ourselves in my bedroom. It's time to get serious and start work.

CHAPTER 30

Just Write

First, we need to decide who's going to write to which teacher. We've got twelve teachers in total, so we agree to divide them equally between us. 'That's six teachers each,' explains Milly, pleased to show off her maths.

We make two lists and pin them up on the wall:

KAYLA
Miss Hillock: games
Mr Champion: geography
Mrs Choon: English
Miss Wurdy: music
Mr Figger: drama
Mr Props: maths

MILLY
Mr Kulla: science
Miss Zinc: art
Mrs Hacker: history
Mr Prior: computer technology
Mrs Parler: cookery
Mr Platter: French

Milly starts writing with impressive energy. 'Easy!' she declares. 'Bet we'll get 'em done in an hour. Then let's binge-watch some movies. The trashier, the better. Serves Mum right for sending that snotty message!' I'm worried that the teachers' notes will take us way longer than that. But I keep quiet and start writing too.

For a while, we make good progress. Milly finishes her first note and I finish my first two. We're using Miss Skipper's big, messy handwriting, and we reckon that our hints and tips are spot-on. Want an example? Here's what Milly writes for science:

Dear Mr Kulla,

I've noticed that your classroom ceiling's covered in goo. I'm sure you'd like to become a better science teacher, with experiments that don't explode. So here's my advice:

1. Don't put anything in a test tube until you've worked out what it is.

2. Then you'll know what you're dealing with.

3. Because different substances behave in different ways. That's why it's science.

4. Don't turn up the heat so high. Check the knob's screwed on properly.

5. In case there's still an explosion, make sure everyone's wearing goggles.

Please use this in your lessons, especially this Friday.

Thank you,

Miss Skipper

PS. No need to talk to anyone about this.

PPS. In fact please keep this note top secret.

My approach is a bit different, but I think it's just as good. Here's my first note:

Hi there Miss Hillock,

Today I spotted you teaching a game of football. May I suggest a few improvements?

1. This game only has two teams, not three.

2. There's only meant to be one ball. Not one ball for each player.

3. It's called football because you kick it. Stuffing it up your T-shirt doesn't count.

4. As the teacher, you're meant to spend more time on your feet than on your bottom. Please practice not tripping up.

5. When a pupil says they're going to start dribbling, don't hand them a tissue. A dribble is a way of moving the ball.

Please don't tell anyone about this note. Please just put it into action. Starting this Friday.

Thanks,

Miss Skipper.

PS: Your pupils really like you, even though your lessons are weird.

Cleo's scratching at the door, miffed at being left out. I let her in, with strict instructions to keep quiet. But she leaps straight onto Milly's lap and knocks the pen out of her hands. 'Oh Kayla!' gushes Milly. 'She's so cute and adorable!'

Those aren't the words I'd use to describe my cat. 'Bossy and big-headed' come more to mind, but Milly doesn't know her as well as I do.

Instead of starting her second note, Milly joins Cleo in a game of pounce-on-the-paper-ball. Followed by a game of build-a-tower (Milly) and knock-it-down (Cleo). I say nothing; I just plough on with my note-writing. But when Cleo and Milly start their third game of hide-and-seek, I can't keep quiet any longer. 'Mills,' I groan. 'You're spoiling her.' Of course what I really mean is 'Since when did cat games help us to save Clods?'

'OK, OK,' sighs Milly. 'I get the hint.' She plonks Cleo in-between Mr Bunnyfun's ears ('Ooh look, Kayla: a furry cat-hat!') and picks up her pen.

I've now finished four of my notes. Milly's still only written one – which she blames on the fact that she's a cat lover. We're both tired, but we have to keep going. No trashy TV for us tonight, after all.

CHAPTER 31

Under Cover

We don't realise how late it is, until Mum and Dad return from the hospital.

Dad runs up to my room. 'Evening, girls. Great to see you both taking your homework so seriously. But you've done enough for today. Time to stop.'

Mum makes up a bed for Milly beneath my desk, which is the only bit of floor space left. Then she reappears with two cups of hot chocolate: 'A special treat, because you've both worked so hard. Drink up, then get ready for bed. No messing about. Lights out in ten minutes.'

As soon as she's gone, Milly and I swap a worried look. I still need to write drama and maths. Milly's even further behind: she still needs to finish art, and she hasn't even started history, computer technology, cookery or French.

'What's the plan now?' she asks me, scooping out the last drips of hot chocolate with her finger.

'We go to bed and switch off the light, like Mum says. Or there'll be trouble.'

'So we give up on the notes?'

'You kidding? Those notes have to get finished. We'll just hide under our duvets and carry on writing.'

'Sorry Kayla, but I can't write in the dark. My eyes aren't magic, y'know!'

'Who needs magic?' I reply, fishing out two little torches, left over from a Christmas cracker. Milly throws me a look of admiration, and I can't help feeling proud of myself.

We make a big display of getting ready for bed, so Mum and Dad don't suspect anything.

'Night, Mum and Dad.'
'Night, Kukoo.'
'Goodnight, Mr and Mrs Grub.'
'Milly love, you can call us Kevin and Krystal.'
'Goodnight, Kevin. Goodnight, Krystal.'
'Goodnight, Milly.'

Now we're both huddled under our duvets with a torch, trying to write our notes. The only problem is, we can't stay awake. 'I can't stop yawning,' whispers Milly from under her duvet. 'My writing's getting slower than a snail.' At least that's what I think she says. It's hard to tell, because the duvets are clamped round our heads.

'Me too,' I whisper back, 'And it's not easy sharing my bed with Mr Bunnyfun.'

'Mmmmffff,' she replies, drowsily.

Eventually, the house goes quiet. Mum and Dad went to bed ages ago, and now all I can hear is Milly's snoring, which means she's writing zero notes.

I switch off my torch, tiptoe over to her bed, and give her a prod. 'Hey Mills, fancy an energy boost? There's a full biscuit tin in the kitchen. If we're really quiet, no one will hear.'

'Whaggh?" she croaks, still half asleep. I trim my message to the essentials: 'Biccies. Kitchen. Now?'

She's still groggy, so I whisper three magic words: 'Choc – chunk – chip.' That does the trick. 'Count me in!' she replies, suddenly wide awake.

CHAPTER 32

Sugar Rush

We creep downstairs, feeling like burglars, which is kind of thrilling. We're pretty good burglars, too: I remember to warn Milly about the creaky bottom stair, and we carefully step over it.

Cleo wants to join in but she's so noisy, I shoo her away. Big mistake: she complains at full volume and clings to my leg. Milly bends down to stroke her, whispering in her ear. 'Cleo, I know you wanna help with the Great Biscuit Robbery. But here's the deal: if you go quietly back to Kayla's room, I promise you another game of hide-and-seek before we go to sleep. How does that sound?'

It works a treat: Cleo falls silent and slinks back upstairs. Trust my cat to prefer my bestie. Typical!

I've taken a gamble on the biscuits: if we're short of money this week, there won't be any choc-chunk-chip ones at all; just boring digestives. And that means Milly will never trust me again. I make a silent wish: 'Please can this be a good money week? Enough for biscuits with any kind of chocolate?' I open the lid and point my torch inside. Yes! Choc-chunk-chip ones, right to the top.

We agree to limit ourselves to six biscuits each. 'Plus one for luck,' grins Milly, grabbing a seventh. Oops: now the tin's so empty, I can see through to the crumbs at the bottom. I rearrange the three biscuits that are left, to try and make it look fuller.

We creep back into the hallway, clutching our biscuits so tight, the choc chunks melt in our hands. But why oh why do we forget about the noisy bottom stair? And why do we both step on it at the same time? CREAK! It echoes through the house, freezing us with fear. If Mum and Dad catch us, those notes will never get finished.

We wait. And wait. Still no sound of Mum and Dad. We got away with it! We sneak up to my room, close the door, and promise each other that we'll be better burglars next time round.

Milly makes an impressive start on her biscuits, whispering in-between the crunching. 'Don't worry, Kayla: we'll soon get those notes sorted. I just need to get this energy boost into my system. In fact if I lie down on your bed it'll get round my body quicker.' She cuddles up to Mr Bunnyfun and promptly falls asleep.

There's no point trying to wake her again; I'll just have to write the rest of her notes myself. I carefully remove the half-eaten biscuit from her hand, cover her with my dressing gown, and switch off her torch.

Cleo realises that she won't get that extra game of hide-and-seek after all. But she's surprisingly grown-up about it. She just curls herself round Milly's feet and dozes off.

Now I'm the only one still awake, and I've never felt so lonely. The clock downstairs is already chiming midnight, and I still need to write six notes: one of mine and five of Milly's. I take a blank sheet of paper, grab my biro, and get started.

When I get to note four, my torch starts to flicker. I switch to Milly's torch and keep going.

Each time I finish a note, I eat a biscuit as a reward. It's getting chilly, but I can't use my dressing gown because it's still wrapped around Milly. I put on my Clods jumper instead, and wrap the skirt around my neck as a scarf. Whatever it takes to keep going.

I finish my last note just after the clock chimes 1am. That means it's already Thursday – the last day before Snoop's visit. But my plan is still on track: the twelve finished notes are piled neatly on my desk, waiting to be dropped into the teachers' bags.

I reach for my sixth and final biscuit, and it tastes the best of all. Wonder what Granny will say when I tell her? Wonder if she's awake right now? I pull back my curtain and look out across town.

Everywhere's dark, except for one tall building with lots of lights on. Maybe that's the hospital? 'Night, Granny,' I whisper, blowing a kiss. 'Thanks for everything. Sleep well.' I creep under my desk and snuggle into the bed that Mum made up for Milly. Within seconds I'm fast asleep.

CHAPTER 33

Safety Pin

'Kukoo! Milly! Wakey wakey!' Mum's standing in my doorway, wrapped in her dressing gown. 'You've slept through your alarm. Anyone would think you two had been up all night. And how come you've ended up in each other's beds? Some kind of game, I suppose.'

She picks some biscuit crumbs off our duvets and gives us suspicious looks. I'm glad we're running late, because she doesn't have time to ask how those crumbs got there. She just says 'breakfast in five minutes' and hurries off to get dressed.

Milly's so tired, she puts on my skirt, instead of hers. 'Hey Kayla, my skirt's got a safety pin. Never noticed it before. Weird or what?' Great. Now I have to explain how rubbish my life is. 'It's not your skirt, Mills. It's mine.'

'OK, but why's it got a safety pin?'

'To stop it falling down.'

'Why don't you just get a skirt that fits properly?'

Where do I begin? I'm ashamed that my school uniform is second-hand and too big. I'm ashamed that my mum and dad don't have enough money. Right now, I'm ashamed to be Kayla Grub.

I feel my cheeks burn when I mumble my reply: 'The skirt needs to be big enough for me to grow into. It works out cheaper that way.'

'But school skirts aren't expensive, Kayla.'

No wonder Milly doesn't get it. She lives in a big posh house on the edge of town and goes skiing every year. Her mum and dad are lawyers.

'Skirts *are* expensive!' I hiss at her. 'Especially if your parents are an Assistant Caretaker and a Chief Washer-Upper!'

Now it's Milly's turn to look ashamed. 'I just didn't think. Sorry.'

She looks really upset, but I'm too worked up to care. 'Which sorry are you?' I snap. 'Sorry that my family are poor? Or sorry that you're too rich to understand?'

'Both, I guess. But y'know what? Your safety pin's really clever. I'd never come up with such a cool trick. So please will you stop being mad at me?'

We finish getting dressed in silence. Deep down, I know it's not Milly's fault; her family's just very different to mine.

Maybe one day I'll unroll my jumper sleeves and show her how they actually hang down to my knees. If that doesn't put her off, I'll show her the scrunched-up newspaper inside my shoes. Then she might begin to know the real Kayla. But I'm not ready for that yet. Not even with my bestie.

She finally cheers up when she reaches inside her washbag and finds one-and-a-half biscuits left over from last night. 'Nice healthy start to the day!' she chuckles, chomping away. As she finishes the last one, her eye catches the twelve finished notes sitting on my desk. 'We did a pretty good job, eh Kayla? Six notes each. What a dream team!'

Has she really forgotten that she only wrote one teeny little note, and I had to write all the others? I don't want to quarrel anymore, so I put all my energy into a nod and smile. Then we head downstairs, reminding each other to act totally normal.

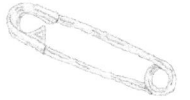

CHAPTER 34

Mrs Mobbs

'Morning, girls!' begins Dad. 'How did the French music go?'

I've no idea what he's talking about. 'French what?'

'Don't say *what*. Say *I beg your pardon*!' shouts Mum from the kitchen.

Dad's not giving up. 'You know: French music. The homework you were telling us about.'

Milly kicks my ankle, which finally jolts me awake. 'Oh, French music! Yeah, thanks Dad. We got it finished in the end.'

'Great. You'll have to show us sometime.'

Mum shouts through from the kitchen. 'It's all part of their Pee-Pee-Pee-Pee-Pee Plan, remember?'

'Tee-Tee-Tee-Tee-Tee Plan' Milly cuts in, firmly. 'Big difference.'

'Really?' replies Mum, coming in with a pile of toast. 'What does it actually stand for?'

Milly freezes, realising she's gone too far. It's not the sort of thing you can lie about on the spot. BEEP BEEP! A car horn honks just outside, grabbing our attention. 'It's my mum,' explains Milly. 'I asked her to come and collect Mr Bunnyfun.'

Is any car big enough for Mr Bunnyfun? I reckon he'll need a whole truck. I peer through the blinds: it's an open-top sports car with only two seats. How on earth will he fit?

Milly's mum must be in a hurry, because she doesn't get out to say hello. She checks her lipstick in the mirror, pats her hair into place, and honks the horn again.

Milly and I manage to squeeze Mr Bunnyfun into the passenger seat. He looks so funny, we can't stop giggling. The rest of the street loves him, too: they cheer and wave as they hurry off to work. But then Mrs Mobbs snaps at Milly for making her late, and it's not fun anymore.

Mum's determined to make friends. She opens the front door and calls across: 'Morning, Mrs Mobbs. Nice to meet you.' But Milly's mum doesn't even notice; she's on the phone, barking orders to one of her secretaries: 'Pick up my dry-cleaning. Get me an oatmilk skinny latte. And don't expect any thanks!'

The minute Mr Bunnyfun is strapped in properly, she glares at Milly and zooms off.

Back inside, Mum wraps our toast in some kitchen roll and hands it over. 'Here you go, girls. You can eat it as you walk to school. It'll save you time. One jam and one marmalade each.' I can't help thinking that my mum's a lot nicer than Mrs Mobbs.

R–! Milly and I reach school just as the bell croaks out its last ring. It's time for the next stage of my plan: to slip our notes into the teachers' bags without being seen – and by the end of today.

There's only problem: I haven't a clue how we'll do it.

CHAPTER 35

Minx Mob

It doesn't start well. Milly and I can't even get through the school entrance, because it's blocked by Trixie and her followers. She's started calling them the Minx Mob, and they're mad enough to let her.

'Well look who it is!' begins Trixie. 'Gut-Face and Frizz-Bucket. Or is that Frizz-Face and Gut-Bucket? Take your pick.'

We try to squeeze past, but the Minx Mob won't budge. 'You both look tired,' sneers Trixie. 'I suppose you've been up all night. Working on your oh-so-secret project.'

I think of the teachers' notes stashed away in my bag, and grab it tight. What a stupid move! Now Trixie's even more suspicious. 'Ooh!' she smirks. 'What's in there, I wonder?'

Milly turns on Trixie. 'Listen up, Stinky-Minx: who cares if that's where we've hidden our secret? You'll never know for sure!' She realises her mistake and claps her hand to her mouth, but it's too late. Trixie turns to the Minx Mob. 'Search Frizz-Face's bag. Now!'

They're not properly trained yet because they hang back, awkwardly. 'That's an order, you cretins!' yells Trixie, pushing them towards me.

Now they reach out for my bag but Milly grabs it too. 'Don't let Stinky-Minx boss you around!' she tells them, gripping my bag with both fists. Somehow the strap's now wound around my neck, choking me. But no one notices; they're locked in their deadly tug-of-war.

'Nice work, Minx Mob!' smirks Trixie. 'Nearly there!'

The strap pulls even tighter. I can't breathe. Everything's gone blurred. I'm going to collapse.

'WHAT ON EARTH'S GOING ON HERE?' bellows Miss Skipper, storming into the playground. The Minx Mob drop my bag like it's on fire, and scuttle back to Trixie. I hold onto Milly, drawing in great lungfuls of air, just glad to be alive.

Miss Skipper plants herself in front of the group, eyeing us all fiercely. 'I will NOT tolerate this shameful behaviour! Clods is many things, but it is not a fight-club! One more slip-up and you'll all be in serious trouble. Do you understand?'

'Yes, Miss Skipper,' we all murmur.

'Louder, please.'

'Yes, Miss Skipper!' we all shout.

She folds her arms, still furious. 'Now go inside. All of you. You're already late for class.'

As we trudge through the front door, Trixie pulls me to one side. 'Don't go thinking it's over, Frizz-Face. I'll sniff out your precious secret, if it's the last thing I do!'

Great. Dropping off the teachers' notes was never going to be easy. But how the hell can we do it, now that Trixie and the Minx Mob are out to get us?

CHAPTER 36

Trip Trick

In the mid-morning break, I spot our first chance. Mr Prior and Mrs Hacker are chatting to each other in the busy corridor. Their bags are slung over their shoulders – and wide open. Best of all, Trixie and the Minx Mob are nowhere to be seen.

'Quick!' I tell Milly. 'Why don't we drop our notes into their bags as we walk past?'

'Ooh, risky!' she warns. 'Bagsy I do Mrs Hacker.'

'Why?'

'Cos she's less likely to spot me.'

'Why?'

'Cos she wears glasses.'

'Isn't the point of glasses to make you see properly?'

'Picky as always, Kayla! Mrs Hacker's note, please!'

I hand her that one, and get ready to drop off my own note with Mr Prior.

We head towards the two teachers, trying to look casual. One more step and we'll be right beside them. Now we're holding the notes over their open bags, ready to drop them in...

'Well hello, you two!' The voice is loud, cheerful and very familiar. It's Mum, on her way to the canteen. She's waving her rubber gloves at us: two bright-pink flags, squeaking as they flap around.

How many times have I begged Mum to ignore me anywhere near school? 'Just pretend I don't exist,' I've told her. It's bad enough being the frizzy-haired girl in the second-hand uniform. The girl with the weird accent. If the other kids find out that both my parents are at Clods too, they'll think I'm a total freak.

And of all the times, why does she have to turn up now?

Quick as a flash, Milly and I stuff the notes up our jumpers. 'Everything OK?' Mum asks, brightly. 'As if!' I think to myself. 'It was fine until *you* came along. Thanks for nothing.' But of course I don't say it out loud.

'Can't stop,' Mum continues. 'Today's lunch is extra-greasy, so I'm making an early start. No harm in showing off my skills, eh Kukoo? That's the way to get on in life!'

'Good luck,' Milly tells her kindly. 'Go show that grease who's boss! Blitz it! Zap it! Knock it dead!' All I can do is mutter 'Kayla, not Kukoo.'

'Well that's gone and blown it,' sighs Milly once Mum's safely out of sight. 'We can't sneak up to those teachers again. It'll look too suspicious.'

I chew my lip thoughtfully. 'What if you distract 'em, so I can drop off the notes without being spotted?'

'Any suggestions?'

'Errr... umm...'

'Easy!' she gloats, 'I've got the perfect plan! Let's go.'

We set off towards the teachers, and once again we're within reach.

'Ooommppphhh!!!!' Without warning, Milly trips, flies through the air and lands sprawling at the teachers' feet. 'Wh-where am I?' she asks them, grabbing their ankles.

They bend down to help her. 'Goodness, Milly Mobbs! That was quite a tumble! Are you OK?' She's heavier than they realised, and the three of them wobble around like a circus act. It's the perfect moment for me to act: in one smooth move, I drop the notes into their bags and walk away.

Milly spots what I've done and finally stands up straight. 'Thanks, Mrs Hacker. Thanks, Mr Prior. I'm fine. Sorry about the ankle-grabbing, but no hard feelings, eh? Gotta dash.'

She runs over to join me, and as soon as we're round the corner, I smugly punch the air. 'Mills, that trip-up was amazing!'

'Cheers hun, but it's not what you think.'

'Huh?'

'I was planning to ask 'em a question about today's timetable. I tripped by accident.'

We laugh so loudly, everyone nearby ends up smiling too. Everyone except Trixie and the Minx Mob. Damn! How long have they been here? What have they seen? What have they heard?

'What's so funny?' Trixie asks me, flicking her half-finished chewing gum into the frizziest bit of my hair.

'Just a private joke,' I reply, yanking at the chewing gum to pull it free. Ouch! It comes loose with a whole handful of my hair and looks gross, sitting there in my hand. The Minx Mob nudge each other and chuckle.

'Liar!' snarls Trixie. 'I saw you getting creepily close to the teachers just now. I suppose that's part of your precious secret?'

Milly steps forward, hands on hips. 'Listen, Minx-Muck: you need your eyes testing. Kayla didn't drop off any notes, and especially not in the teachers' bags!'

The Minx Mob laugh at Milly for giving away the secret so easily.

'Oh Gut-Bucket,' chortles Trixie. 'You're the best. What's so special about those notes, then? What do they say?'

I drag Milly away before she can do any more damage. 'Sorry, Kayla,' she groans. 'I messed up – again!' She looks so miserable, I pretend we're still OK. 'Don't stress, Mills. Yes, Trixie knows about the notes. But she still doesn't know what they're about.'

R–ing! Ri–! R–! Time for our next lesson. We've still got ten more notes to deliver, and there's nothing we can do about it until lunchtime. Even worse: Trixie's already halfway towards discovering our secret.

That laugh in the corridor with Milly feels like a very long time ago.

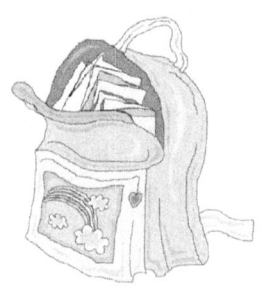

CHAPTER 37

Last Chance

R–ing! Ri–! R–! As soon as the lunch bell goes, we grab a quick sandwich and stuff it down in five minutes flat. That leaves us the rest of the break to scoot along the corridors, looking for a chance to deliver the rest of the notes.

But this time, we're out of luck: our teachers whizz around too quickly, and there's no way we can get to their bags. Plus the Minx Mob are following us every step of the way, trying to catch us out.

'Maybe I could repeat the tripping-up thing?' suggests Milly. 'It's as painful as falling off my pony, but at least it's more useful.'

'Mills, you're awesome. But it's the kind of stunt you can only do once.'

'Not true. The more I do it, the better I'll get.' She pulls up her socks to hide her knees, which are purple with bruises from this morning.

I try to explain it a different way. 'What if the teachers decide you're ill and send you home? How will I manage without you? In any case, we won't fool the Minx Mob. They'll report us to Trixie and she'll report us to Miss Skipper.'

Milly's disappointed but takes it bravely. 'Well it's a shameful waste of my talent. From now on, I'll just have to practice tripping up in private.'

The mid-afternoon break's just as hopeless: none of our teachers are within reach, and the Minx Mob are still hovering round us like a swarm of flies. Those ten notes are still sitting in my schoolbag and I'm getting desperate.

Our last lesson of the day is French with Mr Platter and it's the usual chaos, but for once I barely notice. I write three lines in my notebook:

Task: Ten notes still to deliver today.

Problem: Snoop arrives tomorrow.

Solution: ???

I try writing it in French, in case it helps me to come up with something. But I don't know enough of the words.

'Hey Kayla,' whispers Milly. 'Why are you biting your lip?'

'I'm trying to save the TTTTT Plan from disaster.'

'Phew. I was worried something was wrong.'

Sometimes I can't tell if Milly's joking or not.

R–ing! Ri–! R–! Time to go home. Trixie takes one look at my gloomy face and laughs triumphantly. 'Hey Frizz-Face, whatever you were trying to do, you've failed – ha ha!' She hands out bags of crisps to the Minx Mob and they all head home.

Milly and I trudge along the corridor and she gives me a comforting pat on the back. 'Sorry it didn't work out. We'll just have to wait for Poop-Snoop to close us down. Wanna shoulder to cry on?'

I half-hide my tearful face on her shoulder, but something catches my eye. It's Miss Skipper, pinning a note to the staffroom door:

Teachers' meeting. Starting now.
Who knows? It might even be fun!

An idea hits me like a thunderbolt. Maybe we can drop off the rest of the notes, after all! I spring out of Milly's hug and seize her by the shoulders. 'Hey Mills, remember your fire alarm idea?'

'The idea you said was terrible?'

'Yeah, sorry about that. Actually, it might just work.'

'Well you've changed your tune!'

'Cos the timing's perfect. Everyone's going home, right?'

'Yeah, even Trixie and the Minx Mob.'

'But the teachers are sticking around!'

'How d'you know?'

'Look at that note, Mills. The one Miss Skipper's just pinned to the staffroom door.'

'Oh yeah. Teacher meeting. Big deal.'

'It *is* a big deal, and here's why: if we set off the alarm, the teachers will have to leave the building.'

'So? They'll take their bags with 'em.'

'No, cos when there's a fire, you're meant to get out quickly. Which means leaving your bags behind.'

As this new twist sinks in, she grips me and says 'Blimey!'

'I know! We'll just sneak into the empty staffroom. The teachers' bags will be there, ready for us to deliver the notes!'

'How do we know which bag belongs to which teacher?'

Damn. I hadn't thought of that. But I babble on as though everything's sorted. 'We'll quickly see what's inside each bag and work out who it belongs to. Then we'll put the right note into each bag, and clear off before the fire brigade comes.'

'If we're found out, we're in the biggest trouble of our lives.'

'I know. But will you do it, Mills? This is about saving our school, remember? And saving my Mum and Dad's jobs. So we can stick around and look after Granny Grub. Plus your mum might still let Billy switch to Clods, and we have to give him that chance. We'll never forgive ourselves if we walk away now.'

'I wish I'd never thought of the fire alarm thing,' she sighs. But her eyes are shining and I can tell she's decided to help me.

CHAPTER 38

Smashing Time

I'm standing by the fire alarm just outside the staffroom, and Milly's keeping a lookout to check the corridor's clear. Miss Skipper's meeting has started and everyone else has left.

'OK, now!' hisses Milly in a dramatic whisper. With shaking hands, I unroll one of my stupidly long sleeves to wrap around my fist. Who'd have thought that those sleeves would turn out to be so useful? I clench my fist, punch through the glass, and press the button.

WAO-WAO-WAO-WAO-WAO!!! The alarm's so loud, I feel like it's going to split my head open. Milly and I stick our fingers in our ears and dive for cover behind a bookcase. It's a tiny, cramped space but at least we're hidden – and in-between the shelves, there's a crack that we can peep through.

We watch the staffroom door, scared to blink in case we miss something. We don't have to wait long. The door flies open and the teachers gather outside the staff room, covering their ears and wondering what to do next.

They look grumpy and I'm not surprised: they've already had a long, hard day of being terrible teachers. Miss Skipper comes out last, like a sheepdog herding her flock.

I give Milly a proud thumbs-up, but when I peep through the crack again, my plan comes crashing down. Because now I spot that the teachers have brought their bags with them! What made me so sure that this wouldn't happen? Why am I such a know-it-all?

Milly's spotted it too, and I can tell she's groaning, even though I can't hear it. I mouth the word *sorry!* and I'm expecting her to mouth *told you so!*, but instead she smiles and shrugs. So she doesn't blame me, after all. She's the best friend I've ever had.

What now? Well one thing's clear: my plan has failed – already. All we can do now is try to escape without being seen.

We're still waiting to set off, when someone appears at the far end of the corridor, running towards the staffroom. They're carrying a mop, and wearing freshly ironed caretaker's overalls, topped with a gleaming badge.

Yes, it's Dad. Which means that things have just got even more complicated.

CHAPTER 39

Fireman Dad

Why's Dad carrying a mop? Maybe he thinks it can put out the fire? In the meantime it's dripping water onto his boots.

He shouts to be heard above the din. 'Ladies and gents, please leave the building quickly, and I must insist that you leave your bags behind!'

The teachers don't like being ordered around. They start to complain: 'Now look here, Mr Grub –'

Dad interrupts them. 'Come along folks, you know the rules. Your bags will slow your escape.'

Some of them still won't give in. 'Where's Miss Skipper? We demand a second opinion.'

Dad waves his mop at them. 'You can demand all you like, but I'm sure that Miss Skipper will agree with me. So please drop your bags this second. Then leave the building by the nearest fire exit.'

Miss Skipper steps forward, and her voice is surprisingly loud when she makes the effort. 'Thank you, Mr Grub. You're right, of course. Let's drop our bags right here, and flee this dreadful noise.'

The teachers realise they're no match for Dad and Miss Skipper. But they make their point by taking their bags back into the staffroom, rather than dumping them in the corridor. They reappear bag-free, and head to the fire escape. Some of them glare at Dad on their way out, but he stands his ground.

Milly and I grin at each other, amazed at this turnaround. Dad's forced the teachers to dump their bags! He's rescued our plan, without even knowing! Now we just need him to follow the teachers out of the building, so we can dive into the staffroom and deliver our notes.

But this time Dad drives us crazy, because he doesn't leave. Despite the deafening fire alarm, he starts checking the whole damn corridor, in case he's missed someone. He searches behind doors and under tables. He pulls back curtains, lifts up chairs and even peers under a mat. What if he checks behind our bookcase? He'll find Milly and me, and it'll be the end of life as we know it.

Oh my god, it's happening! He's spotted our bookcase and he's rushing towards us! We curl up as small as we can, but if Dad takes one step nearer, there's no way he'll miss us. We hold our breath, clench our bottoms, and start counting: one... two...

'Mr Grub, can you hear me? Can I make a suggestion?' That's Miss Skipper's voice. We dare to uncurl ourselves and look through the crack again.

She's standing at the fire escape, shouting across to Dad. 'You've done a truly heroic job, Mr Grub, but please don't risk your own life any longer. Do come and join us outside, whilst we await the fire brigade.'

After a painfully long pause, Dad nods and runs over to join her. He helps her onto the fire escape, takes one last look around, and disappears out of sight.

Finally! Now Milly and I can put our plan into action. I tap her on the shoulder, point towards the staffroom and mouth 'Let's get in there!'

CHAPTER 40

In the Bag

We run into the staffroom, our hands still clamped to our ears. WAO-WAO-WAO-WAO-WAO!!! The alarm's so loud in here, we can barely think. But we know what to do: drop off the notes and get out fast.

I seize the first bag and yank it open. Inside, there's an inflatable globe, punctured by drawing pins. That's bound to be Mr Champion, our geography teacher. I stuff his note inside and move on. The next bag's tangled up with guitar strings. That means music and Miss Wurdy. Another note delivered.

Milly works speedily through the bags on the other side of the room. Whenever she's not sure, she shows the bag to me and I mouth an answer.

Gooey goggles = science = Mr Kulla.
Jammy apron = cookery = Mrs Parler.
Muddy whistle = games = Miss Hillock.

We've only got two notes and two bags to go: Miss Zinc (art) and Mr Props (maths). But which bag's which? It's hard to tell. In a fit of rage, Milly flings them across the room. One of the bags does a somersault and something falls out: the paintbrush that Miss Zinc puts through her hair. Perfect! This bag is Miss Zinc's, and the other one is Mr Props'.

I drop in the final two notes and shoot Milly a look that says 'Let's get out of here!'

But we've barely reached the door, when the fire alarm does something even more terrifying: it stops! WAO-WAO-WAO!!!... silence. Then more silence. Followed by yet more silence. We freeze like statues, caught off guard.

The creepy stillness is broken by a man's voice. It's Dad, speaking to the teachers in the playground just outside. 'Good news, folks: turns out there's no fire, after all. That's why I've stopped the alarm.'

We inch towards the window and peep through the blinds. Miss Skipper steps forward. 'Thank you, Mr Grub. Good news indeed. But are you sure?'

He nods confidently. 'I popped back into the corridor, just now – and noticed something strange.'

'What did you see?' demand the teachers eagerly. 'Footprints? A burnt-out cigarette? A shady figure, running away?'

'No, it was the fire alarm by the staffroom. Its glass cover is smashed to pieces.'

'Goodness!' gasps Miss Skipper. 'So the alarm wasn't triggered by smoke, after all? Someone deliberately set it off? But who?'

The teachers start blaming each other, until they realise that it couldn't be any of them, as they were all together in the staffroom. They pipe down again and look to Dad for an answer.

He breaks the news gently. 'Sorry to say this, folks, but the culprit seems to be a Clods pupil.'

'Surely not!' exclaims Miss Skipper, with a cry that goes straight to my heart.

"Fraid so,' replies Dad. 'Because look what I found, snagged on the broken glass.' He holds out something towards her. It's a long strand of wool, in a familiar shade of muddy brown. I unroll my sleeve, knowing what I'm going to find but dreading it anyway. Yes, a long piece of thread's missing.

'Oh dear,' wails Miss Skipper. 'The culprit was wearing a Clods jumper. One of my pupils, as you say.' She fingers the thread and hands it back to him. 'But why would any Clods pupil do something so stupid?'

'Maybe they were just fooling around? It's no excuse, I know.'

'No excuse at all!' she declares, her voice choking with emotion. 'If there's one thing I was proud of, it's that every pupil cares about Clods as much as I do. But it seems I was mistaken.'

'Perhaps we'll never find out who's behind it,' answers Dad softly. 'But most of the Clods kids do you proud, Miss Skipper. Kids like my Kayla.'

'True,' she replies wistfully. 'Kayla's such a credit to this school. No wonder you and Mrs Grub are so proud of her. I just wish that more of my pupils could follow her example.' I fight back tears, wishing I could be the person they think I am.

Miss Skipper turns to the teachers. 'Well I think we've all had quite enough excitement for one day. You'll be relieved to know that our staff meeting's cancelled. I suggest we collect our bags and go home.'

Now my heartbreak turns to panic. Milly and I are still trapped in the staffroom, and the teachers are coming back to collect their bags! There's no escape. We're doomed!

CHAPTER 41
Hide-Away

The teachers' footsteps are getting louder. They're back in the corridor and heading to the staffroom. Which makes the staffroom the very last place where Milly and I want to be. If you asked us right now to choose between the staffroom and a creepy dungeon, we'd choose the dungeon and count ourselves lucky.

We have to hide. But where? We frantically look around the room. A-ha: the coat stand! It's heaped with the teachers' coats, and big enough for both of us. We leap behind it and huddle together, then I jump straight out again.

'Wassup?' hisses Milly, peeping out in-between an anorak and a puffer jacket.

'It won't work, Mills! The teachers will take their coats, and we'll be left trying to hide behind a pole.'

'Damn it, Kayla! Why can't you be wrong for once?'

There's only one place left: the lost property cupboard, full of dirty games kit. We leap inside, crouch down and pull the door shut.

'Stinks in here!' groans Milly. 'What the hell are we sitting on?' I'm trying to explain that it's sweaty football socks, when a bra falls from a coat-hanger onto our heads. We stuff our knuckles into her mouths, to stop ourselves giggling. How could anyone manage to lose their bra... at school?

The teachers are back, and chatting away.

'That's funny; I could've sworn that I left my bag on the other chair.'

'Me too.'

'Although we did leave in a hurry. So maybe I've remembered it wrong.'

'Yes, I suppose that explains it.'

'Thank goodness tomorrow's Friday!'

'Indeed. Let's hope it's a nice quiet one, eh?'

If only they knew! With Snoop coming tomorrow, 'nice and quiet' is the very last thing that's going to happen. Their footsteps disappear down the corridor. Then silence again.

'Can we open up, now?' whispers Milly. 'Those stinky socks are heating up beneath my bottom and it's making 'em even stinkier.'

'Maybe we should wait a bit longer?'

'Kayla, please let me out right now, or I'll throw up.'

'OK, good plan.'

We're about to open the cupboard door when we hear a pair of clumpy boots and a rattle of keys. I groan and hide my head in my hands.

'Wassup?' hisses Milly again. 'Who is it?'

'It's Dad, coming to lock up the staffroom.'

Now Milly groans too. 'But we'll be locked in here all night! Our parents will think we're missing and they'll call the police and –'

CLINK. Dad locks the staffroom door and walks away. We crawl out of the cupboard, feeling like we've been trapped in there for days.

Milly finally realises that she's got a pair of underpants draped over her shoulder, and I honestly think she's going to vomit with disgust. I somehow find the nerve to pull them off her and throw them back in the cupboard.

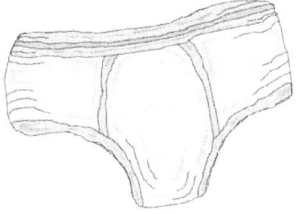

'Gross!' I mutter, wiping my hand on my skirt. Milly gulps down some air. 'Yeah, remind me never to enter that cupboard again.'

We give ourselves a shake and ask each other the same question: 'Now what?'

'Any ideas?'

'Nope. You?'

'Nope.'

'In that case, Mills, can I borrow your phone?'

'Sure, but why?'

'Cos we're out of options. I'll have to call Dad and ask him to come and let us out.'

She grips my arm. 'But he'll know that the fire alarm was down to us!'

'Yeah, and I guess he'll need to hand us over to the police. But if we stay here much longer, our parents will report that we're missing, and the police will come looking for us, anyway. You said so, yourself.'

She sniffs back a tear. 'I don't wanna go to prison! The food's horrible!'

'Look, if we're lucky, they might let us out after a few years.'

'Waah!' Her tear becomes a downpour, so I try another tack. 'Hey Mills, when you're in prison, your mum'll miss you loads. She'll realise how much she loves you.'

That stops her tears, but she still looks serious. 'Kayla,' she begins calmly. 'Now that we're going to prison, we might never see each other again. So there's something I need to say.'

My mouth goes dry. She's going to tell me that I've ruined her life. And she's right: it's my mad plans that have got us into this mess. 'I already know I'm an idiot!' I blurt out. 'And I'm gutted that I've dragged you down with me.'

'What are you talking about?' she frowns.

'Mills, you've got every right to hate me. And –'

'Kayla!' she snaps. 'Will you please stop babbling, and hear me out? I've got a confession to make.'

I'm stunned into silence.

'It's about the teachers' notes,' she continues. 'I knew all along that I only wrote one of 'em. I knew that you had to do all the others. But I claimed that I'd done my fair share. I was pretending to be as clever as you, just to see what it felt like. But of course it didn't work, cos deep down I knew it was a lie.'

'Clever's not everything,' I sniff. 'Friends are.'

She hands over her phone with a wise nod, and I dial Dad's number.

CHAPTER 42:

Wriggly Window

My call to Dad starts to go through but then fizzles out. I can't get a signal.

'Try going over to the window?' suggests Milly.

Hey, the window opens, right at the top! Why didn't I notice that before? I do my first victory dance in a very long while. 'Mills, you're a genius! You've found escape route. Up there, see?'

She shakes her head. 'It's way too small. You'll get through, cos you're skinny. But me? No way. D'you know what Billy calls me?'

'No. What?'

'Dumpling.'

'Huh?'

'Meaning I'm a bit on the round side.'

'Woah! Harsh.'

'If only. Who had five slices of pizza last night? Me. And biscuits this morning before breakfast? Me again.'

'Look, even if you're still full of pizza and biscuits, you *will* squeeze through. I'll go first, so I can pull you outside. And if you fall, I'll catch you.'

'Promise?'

'Promise.' I climb onto the window sill, heave myself up to the opening, and wriggle through the gap.

Remember that certificate I earned at Peach Primary: *Best Leap from a Trampoline onto a Pile of Cushions*? Maybe this is the moment I was training for.

Soon, I'm dangling on the outside of the window, and clinging to the ledge. I just need to let go, so I can drop down into the playground. Ready, steady – OWWW!!! I fall into the prickliest rosebush that's ever been invented.

Crying inside, I sit up and survey the damage: a ripped uniform, scratched legs, and hair that's stuffed with leaves. The rosebush looks even worse: it's now bent and twisted, its yellow petals scattered everywhere.

'You OK, hun?' asks Milly, anxiously watching me from the other side of the window, her face pressed against the glass.

'Sure!' I lie, spitting out a twig. I scramble to my feet and brush the mud off my skirt. 'Trust me, Mills: it's way easier than it looks!'

'OK then, here goes.' She starts squeezing herself through the gap, somehow ending up backwards: her legs and bottom are dangling outside, but her top half is still in the staffroom. Even though no one's watching,

I hold her skirt in place to stop her knickers showing. A girl needs her dignity, always and everywhere.

'You're doing great, Mills! Just wiggle a bit more, then I'm ready to catch you.'

'Can't.'

'Why?'

'Why d'you think? I'm stuck. See? I *told* you I'm a dumpling!' She kicks her legs frantically, but the rest of her doesn't budge. 'You go on without me,' she declares bravely. 'I'll just wait here and figure out a plan.'

'Such as?'

'I plan to get hungry very soon. That'll make me a bit thinner. Thin enough to squeeze through.'

'Have you ever been that hungry before?'

'Nope.'

'Then we can't risk it. Extreme hunger's a dangerous thing. You never know what might happen.'

I pick my way back into the remains of the rosebush – OW! – grab her legs, and gently pull her free. She wriggles out inch by inch, then – 'AAARRKKK!!!' – falls towards me.

I've no idea how the next bit happens, but she lands right on top of me, crushing me into the ground. 'Cheers!' she tells me, happily bouncing to her feet. 'You're a surprisingly comfy pillow!'

I manage to reply 'No probs!' instead of 'That was agony!'

How many thorns are sticking into me, right now? Too many to count. I stagger up and pull the prickly stalks out of my clothes, biting my lip to distract me from the pain.

Milly doesn't notice; she's looking for the next stage of our escape. 'So now we just sprint to the side-gate?' she asks, limbering up like an athlete.

'Yep. Ready?'

'Now or never!'

We run as if our lives depended on it. If Dad's still around, this is where we'll be spotted. With every step, we expect him to shout 'Kukoo? Milly? What's going on?' But no one shouts anything.

We sprint through the side-gate and don't stop until we're several blocks away from the scene of our crime.

CHAPTER 43

High Street

Safe at last! When we reach the high street, we clutch a lamppost to catch our breath.

'We did it!' gloats Milly. 'That was more thrilling than a theme park. Cheaper, too! And no queues! Just a shame there wasn't any ice cream.' She finally notices my uniform and gasps with surprise. 'Oh no: look at you!' She flips me round to inspect all the rips and holes, and scrapes some mud off my back.

'Cheers, Mills. I guess the rosebush came off worse.'

'So how come *my* uniform looks OK?'

It's because she landed on top of me, of course. But I don't want her to feel bad about it, so I don't say anything. She's worried enough, as it is. 'What'll your parents say, Kayla? I guess they can't afford to buy you a new uniform?'

'I'll just have to fix it without 'em knowing.'

'Wow! Didn't realise you're a sewing whizz.'

'I'm not.'

She gives me a pitying smile and we set off home, along the high street.

We weren't planning to stop at Ink-Spot (the tattoo parlour), but when we glance through the window, we spot someone shockingly familiar. He's sitting with the other customers and trying to act normal, even though he's years younger than the rest of them.

We storm inside and Milly grabs him by the shoulders. 'Billy, you've gotta be joking. A tattoo?'

'You can't stop me, Sis – so save your breath and leave me alone.'

'I suppose this is the next stage of your protest?'

'Yeah, and it's a game-changer!'

'You really think that inking your body will make Mum switch you to Clods?'

'Wait till you see what I'm planning!'

He holds out his hands, to show us the message he's already applied with a biro. One hand says *I DEMAND* and the other hand says *REEDOM!* I think he means *freedom*, but now isn't the time to nit-pick.

'Maybe I should ask 'em to slap it on my forehead?' he continues. 'Then Mum'll really notice!'

'That revolting message isn't going anywhere near you!' scowls Milly, yanking him out of his seat and pulling him outside.

'Anything to escape Swindel!' he growls, pulling free and charging back to the door.

'You realise it's illegal?' I call out after him.

He swivels round. 'Excuse me?'

'You can't get inked till you're eighteen. You're under-age, Billy. The tattooist will take one look at you and throw you out.'

He slams his fists together. 'Damn it! I'll just have to go back to scratching my skin with a pin. Trouble is, it doesn't last long enough. My SWINDEL SUCKS message vanished a few days ago, cos the scab went crusty and fell off.'

Milly clenches her teeth. 'No more blood. No more scabs. Please, Bruv. I beg you!'

'Oh, don't you worry,' he frowns. 'I'll find another way... or else!' He finally notices my trashed uniform and forgets his own problems for a second. 'Blimey, Kayla: what happened to *you*? Going for the rough-and-tumble look? Suits you, by the way.' He briefly grins, more like his usual self.

I can't face any more questions. 'See you tomorrow!' I reply, turning away and breaking into a run. But the sprint turns out to be my next mistake, because a few corners later, I run straight into Trixie. She's coming out of the Snack-Attack store, carrying a huge multipack of crisps.

I try to swerve past her but it's too late: I bump into her, sending her flying. She lands on top of the multipack, and the crisp packets burst open: BANG, BANG, BANG! We glare at each other in deadly silence, and even though she's my enemy, I find myself going to pick her up.

'Get your filthy hands OFF me!' she snaps, staggering to her feet and smoothing down her glossy pony-tail. I go to scoop up the crisps instead but that makes her even madder. 'Leave them, you pathetic excuse for a human being! They were only for the Minx Mob anyway, so who cares?'

Just like Billy, she finally notices the shocking state of my clothes. But her reaction couldn't be more different: she gloats with delight. 'Ooh, what have you been up to? Rolling around in a pigpen? Something to do with your precious secret, I suppose?'

There's no point arguing with her, and I need to get home anyway. I set off again, walking as fast as I can.

But I can still hear her calling out after me. 'You looked a total freak to start with. Now you're just a joke! Do yourself a favour, Frizz-Face: go flush yourself down the toilet!'

She carries on yelling at me, but now I'm too far away to hear. I've got bigger things to worry about than being bullied by Trixie. I need to get home and pretend that it's just been a normal day.

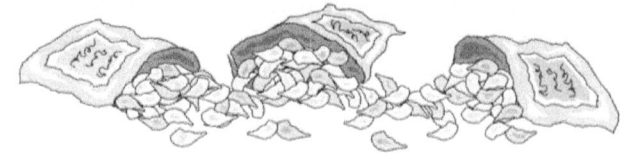

CHAPTER 44

Me and Mum

I open our front door, hoping to creep upstairs and change out of my wrecked uniform before anyone sees it. But Cleo scampers towards me, yelling out a greeting that's loud enough to be heard streets away. Good old Cleo: guaranteed to let me down, every time.

Even so, I might have got away with it if I hadn't stepped onto the creaky bottom stair. Damn! It's even louder than Cleo.

'Is that you, Kukoo?' Mums calls out from the kitchen. 'How was your day? Come and say hello. I've got lots to tell you.'

I pretend I haven't heard her, and start to head upstairs. But she bursts into the hallway, drags me into the living room, plonks me down on the sofa and launches in, barely stopping to breathe.

'Well Kukoo, you remember today's greasy lunch? Of course you do; you probably ate it. Anyway, I wasn't going to let that grease get the better of me. So I did the high-energy scrubbing that I save for emergencies. And d'you know what? Mrs Vittle the Head of Canteen came over to me and said *That's fine work you're doing there, Mrs Grub. How did we ever manage without you? If you carry on like that, we'll be promoting you to dinner lady*. A dinner lady, Kukoo! Me! It's more money *and* a special hat and apron!'

I let her cuddle me as though I was a little kid – even though my face ends up pressed into her boobs. It's difficult to speak into all that booby-ness, but I manage to mumble 'Nice one, Mum!'

Then things get even more awkward. It was bound to happen the first time she noticed me properly. 'Goodness Kukoo, why are your clothes such a mess? Whatever happened?' She sits me straight again and surveys me like I'm some sort of shipwreck.

I put on my innocent face. 'Milly and I stopped off in the park, just now. We got carried away, just mucking about.' I can't believe how easily my lies come, now. The more I do it, the better I get. I'm not sure how this makes me feel.

But it turns out to be a bad lie, because it makes Mum mad. 'And you wonder why we still call you Kukoo? It's because you *behave* like a Kukoo, young lady! A grown-up Kayla would never go and ruin her clothes like that.'

'Hey, that's not fair!'

'Really?' she snorts. 'What kind of game were you and Milly playing? Drag each other through a hedge? Roll around in the mud? Beat yourself up with a tree branch? I can't send you to Clods tomorrow looking like that. You've given me hours and hours of mending, thank you very much. I'll just have to do it this evening, once I'm back from visiting Granny.'

We're still glaring at each other when the front door opens and Dad comes in.

'Never mind me,' Mum tells him as he kisses her forehead. 'Just look at the mess Kukoo's made of her uniform. Apparently our daughter can't visit a park without picking a fight with a badly-behaved tree.'

'Can't be helped, eh Kukoo?' he winks at me, flopping down into the armchair. 'The trees in this town are a pretty violent lot.'

'Well thanks for your support!' she snaps at him. 'And why are you so late?'

'Some idiot set off the fire alarm for a joke, so I stayed behind to help sort it out.'

'Oh no, Kevin! Who'd do such a stupid thing?'

'Wish I knew. Because if I ever get hold of them, I'll –'

I bolt into the kitchen. 'Just grabbing a drink,' I tell them, closing the door behind me.

Cleo's followed me in, watching me closely. She's already guessed that I'm the fire alarm criminal, but will Mum and Dad guess too?

'Don't you dare tell 'em,' I warn her grimly. 'Or you'll never sleep on my bed again. Is that clear?' She shivers at the thought, so I reckon I can trust her to keep quiet.

There's only so long I can spend making a glass of squash, no matter how slowly I run the tap. I add a couple of ice cubes to buy myself some extra time, but now I can't put it off any longer. I grab my drink and head back into the living room, wondering how long it'll take them to find me out.

145

CHAPTER 45

Dreaded Thread

They're still going on about the fire alarm: the damage, the expense, the disruption. Dad's showing Mum the long thread of wool, explaining how he found it and why it matters.

She inspects it closely, admiring his detective work. 'So let me check I've understood: if you can find which Clods pupil this thread belongs to, you've found your criminal?'

'Spot-on, Krystal: the clue's right there, in your hands. Maybe the criminal even had an accomplice. These kids like to work in pairs.' He turns to me. 'Any ideas, Kukoo? Did you notice any kids hanging around the staffroom, just after home-time?'

'M-me?' I stammer. 'No way. 100% not.' Oh, why do I choose this moment to fiddle with my ripped sleeve? It's the stupidest thing I could do, because it makes the rip even worse - and now some woolly brown threads are hanging off. I reach for my drink, sipping it slowly so I can hide my sleeve behind the glass.

Mum goes back to inspecting the thread. 'Well whoever it was, they've gone and ruined a perfectly good jumper. What will their parents say?' She hands it back to Dad and he carefully drops it into my Peach Primary trophy on the mantelpiece. 'Let's keep it there for now,' he says. 'I'll need to hand it over to Miss Skipper if she decides to involve the police.'

KURRGHH! – KURRGHH! – KURRGHH! I choke on my drink and some of it splutters out of my nose. 'How many times must I tell you?' sighs Mum, handing me a tissue. 'Don't guzzle! It's not ladylike. I bet no one ever guzzles at Mrs Mobbs' house.'

I wipe my eyes and blow my nose and hand the soggy tissue back to Mum.

'There's a final twist,' continues Dad. 'Guess what I noticed, just before I left? The staffroom window was open, and the rosebush outside was flattened.'

'Meaning?' asks Mum, burning with curiosity.

'Rosebushes don't destroy themselves,' he replies knowingly. 'The fire alarm idiots must've hidden in the staffroom and escaped through the window. The rosebush got in their way.'

'Ouch!' I chip in, feeling that I ought to say something. At least this time I'm telling the truth; I've got the secret cuts and bruises to prove it.

'Well I feel sorrier for the rosebush,' says Mum. 'What a waste!'

Dad nods solemnly. 'That rosebush was planted by Miss Skipper herself, and she loved it. Remember those superb yellow roses in her office? There'll be no more for her to enjoy, now.'

'Those kids are vicious vandals,' declares Mum. 'No heart. No morals. Caring for no one but themselves!'

'True. If only they were more like our Kukoo, eh? I mentioned that to Miss Skipper and she agreed.'

'Hmm,' frowns Mum. 'Miss Skipper wouldn't agree, if she could see Kukoo right now. Just look at that uniform!'

They give me a searching, disappointed look that makes my palms go sweaty. Will they finally piece it together: the woolly thread, the flattened rosebush... and my trashed clothes? I make a desperate attempt to change the subject. 'Hey Mum, what about the *nice* news? Why don't you tell Dad what Mrs Vittle said about your career skills?'

Amazingly, it works. Her eyes shine with pride and she launches back into the story of her grease-busting triumph. The perfect excuse for me to escape upstairs and get changed.

When I get back down again, they're celebrating Mum's success with a cuppa and wishing that Granny could be here to share the excitement.

'Kukoo, you have the cleverest mum in the world!' proclaims Dad. 'And actually, I've got a little success of my own to report, too.'

Mum sits bolt upright. 'Really, Kevin? Do tell!'

'Miss Skipper was really pleased with how I handled the fire alarm situation. She told me that the Head Caretaker, Mr Hawk, is due to retire soon, and she hopes I'll apply for his job. Not bad, eh?'

Mum's eyes fill with happy tears. 'At last!' she cries. 'Didn't I always say that Clods would recognise our talents? We're finally getting somewhere. It's the chance we've worked so hard for, all these years!'

'Cheers!' They clink their mugs together and do a smoochy kiss. I busy myself in tidying up Cleo's toys, humming a loud tune so I don't have to hear any slurping.

I'm relieved when Dad finally pulls away from her. 'Let's go and share the good news with Granny. Maybe it's the boost she needs to make her well again. If we catch the next bus, she'll still be awake when we arrive.'

They grab their coats and bags, and Mum puts on some lipstick because she's feeling positive about herself and happy with life in general. Dad watches her fondly then suddenly clicks his fingers and turns to me. 'Oh sorry, Kukoo: I forgot to ask about the French music. How did it go?'

'French music?' I echo stupidly, just like last time.

Mum rolls her eyes, which isn't easy when you're applying lipstick. 'Honestly Kukoo! It's what you and Milly were telling us about. You spent yesterday evening doing the homework.'

'Oh yeah!'

'So how did it go?'

'Actually, it was quite noisy and painful. But we muddled through.'

Dad gives me a cheery pat on the shoulder. 'I'd love to take a look, sometime. If I'm going to be Head Caretaker, I ought to keep on top of that sort of thing.'

They trot down the front path, looking ready to conquer the world.

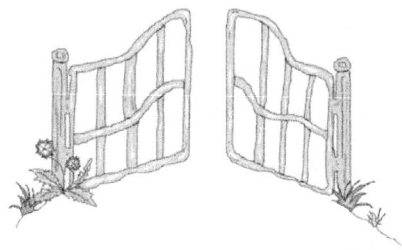

I close the door behind them and turn to Cleo. 'Well girl, we've got one hell of a job to do this evening. Even the worst criminals don't expect their mum to mend their school uniform. The sooner we start, the better.'

CHAPTER 46

Sew Tricky

I lay out my uniform on my bed to inspect it, and count forty-two rips. That rosebush didn't give up without a fight.

Cleo's meant to be helping, but instead she's scampering around my feet. 'Pest!' I yell, bending down to shove her away. That's when I spot what she's playing with: a pile of yellow rose petals! They must have fallen out of my uniform when I got changed.

Those petals are a dead give-away. If Mum and Dad spot a single petal around here, they'll know that I fell into the rosebush. Which means I hid in the staffroom. Which means I set off the alarm. Which means I'm in big trouble.

First things first: I apologise to Cleo. 'You were only trying to warn me,' I tell her. 'You've saved my life.' She milks the situation for all it's worth, demanding that I stroke her ears and say how clever she is, ten times over.

When she's finally satisfied, I get on with wiping those petals from the face of the earth. I start by crushing each petal into a mushy paste. Next, I squash the mess into my glue-pot, then give it a good shake, so the mess mixes into the glue. Annoyingly it fills the glue with dirty streaks, but I guess that's a small price to pay.

Now I can make a start on mending my uniform. But will Cleo allow me to fetch the sewing kit from Granny's wardrobe? She's clearly not happy about it, because she's jumping around to say 'Don't do it! You'll end up looking at Granny's necklace and note, all over again. Then you'll hate yourself for spying.'

'Look,' I tell her sternly. 'I won't even think about those other things. See? I haven't even said 'em out loud. I'll just grab the sewing kit, and pretend those other things aren't there.'

She paws at me to say 'Pathetic! You're fooling yourself!'

'Oh really?' I scoff. 'Well you just watch me, cos I'm about to prove you wrong!'

I go to Granny's wardrobe, pull out the sewing kit, and close the doors again with a proud 'Ha!'

Now I'm meant to walk away, but even though Cleo's watching me through narrowed eyes, I can't resist one more snoop. In a flash of inspiration, I suggest a compromise. 'Hey Cleo, what if I just *touch* those two secret things, and don't actually look? That doesn't count, does it?'

I clamp my eyes shut, open the doors again, and reach into Granny's bottom drawer. Yes, the necklace is exactly where I left it. I feel along the chain until I reach the key, tracing its pattern with my fingertips. I don't even peep at the label, even though I'm desperate to check it still says *For Kayla*.

Without opening my eyes, I reach out to Granny's cardigan pocket. Yes, the note's still there too. I run my fingers across the envelope, as though they could read the actual words: *For Kayla. For when I've gone.*

With heroic self-control, I manage to shut the doors again, before finally opening my eyes. 'See?' I tell Cleo. 'I didn't look at 'em. And I still don't know why Granny's keeping 'em secret. So it's not a cheat, at all. And by the way, why am I justifying myself to a cat?'

Back in my bedroom, I get down to the mending, and turn out to be better at sewing than I expected. Maybe I've got what Granny calls a 'hidden talent'. Just a shame that her mud-coloured cotton is a different shade of mud to my uniform. Who knew that mud was so varied?

Now I've just got to mend the long rip on my sleeve, and it's the biggest rip by far. Will Granny's cotton give me away, here? Will it say *Hey, look what happens when you smash into fire-alarm glass*?

I turn to Cleo for help. 'Any ideas, O Great One?' With a smug flick of her tail, she leads me downstairs and gazes up at my Peach Primary trophy. Of course: that's where Dad dropped the woolly thread! I can simply steal it back again, and use it to mend the rip! It's the perfect match.

Cleo begins her very own victory dance: a series of jumps that should only be tackled by cats half her age. She's forgotten one thing, though: what will Mum and Dad say when they spot that the thread's missing?

'Hey Cleo,' I tell her happily. 'I'll pretend that you jumped onto the mantelpiece and stole the wool to play with. That way, they won't suspect me at all.'

She stops dead and gives me a look that says I'm her worst enemy. I try to reason with her, even though she's turned herself round so I'm talking to her bottom. 'Sorry, Cleo; I know you'll get the blame. You might even be punished. But why are we doing it? To keep Clods open! Then we'll all be here for Granny when she comes out of hospital. Trust me: you'll thank me in the end.'

I take the woolly thread, mend my sleeve, then knock over everything on the mantelpiece so it looks like she's run riot.

I'm too tired to wait for Mum and Dad to get home, so I scribble a note and stick it to the kitchen door:

Thanks for not going mental about my uniform. Not much, anyway. I've mended it myself but don't worry: I've used Granny's muddy cotton.

When I climb into bed, I'm already yawning. It's been the longest, toughest day of my life, but I've survived. I'm still here. I fall asleep with the noise of the alarm still ringing in my ears. It even drowns out the gross things that Trixie yelled at me. And the sound of poor Billy smashing his fists together. All I hear is one long wail: WAO-WAO-WAO-WAO-WAO!!!

CHAPTER 47

Snoop Day

Early next morning, I awake with a start: Snoop visits today!

When I go down for breakfast, Mum's tidying the mantelpiece that I wrecked last night and Dad's searching under the sofa. 'What's up?' I ask them, trying to look innocent. Dad struggles to his feet. 'Your wretched cat's gone and stolen that thread.'

'At least she didn't break anything,' adds Mum, turning my trophy the right way up.

'Yes, but where's the thread now?' he grumbles. 'If Miss Skipper finds out I've lost it, I reckon I've lost my chance to be Head Caretaker!'

I swallow hard. Have I gone and trashed Dad's career, on top of everything else? Now Mum's upset too, and throws herself into his arms. 'Oh Kevin, could Miss Skipper really be so cruel? After all your hard work! And just when we were finally getting somewhere!'

Dad jabs his finger savagely at Cleo. 'No treats for a week, d'you hear me? And I hope you take the time to reflect on the damage you've done to this family!'

Cleo glares at me, meowing furiously. I'm glad no one else understands what she's saying, because it's not pretty. To summarise: our whole house is in a bad mood. Dad's mad at Cleo. Mum's mad at Miss Skipper. Cleo's mad at me. I'm mad at myself. And it's only 8am.

Mum inspects my uniform, determined to say something positive for a change. 'Well done, Kukoo! The stitching shows up a bit, but it's as good as new.'

'Not true, Mum: it was never new to start with. It was second-hand.' That's mean of me, but I can't help it. Mum disappears into the kitchen, upset all over again, and I grab a bowl of cornflakes, feeling even crosser with myself.

Then Dad comes over to join me, and the situation becomes a fully-blown crisis. Because when I glance down at my cornflakes, something shocking is sitting on top: a bright yellow rose petal! It must have fallen out of my jumper, just now. I thought I'd got rid of every last petal, but I was wrong.

Before Dad can spot it, I quickly scoop it up and gulp it down. I just hope it's not poisonous.

R–ing! Ri–! R–! I reach school just in time to see a big posh car sweep through the gates. The number plate says SNOOP 1. That's a pretty big clue, then. Plus there's a window sticker saying *Watch Out, Because I'm Watching You!* So it's official: the Snoop has landed. The car pulls into Miss Skipper's parking space, running over the *Headteacher* sign and smashing it to pieces.

Snoop climbs out and checks his appearance in the wing mirror. He seems pleased with what he sees, but I've no idea why. His suit is as shiny as an oil slick, and his tie's fastened down with a pin that probably doubles up as a weapon.

He smooths down his little moustache and arranges a few strands of greasy hair over the top of his shiny bald head. Smiling at his reflection, he settles a pair of glasses on the end of his long nose. Then he marches to the main door, ready for battle and determined to win.

Milly runs over to join me. 'He looks like a Snoop. He acts like a Snoop. And he's barely even started!'

For once, I don't have an answer.

'You OK?' asks Milly, worried.

'Depends whether rose petals are poisonous.'

'Blimey! Why d'you ask?'

'I ate one for breakfast.'

'Couldn't your family afford any food?'

'Doh! It fell out of my jumper, into my cornflakes.'

'Ooh, dangerous! Well if you start foaming at the mouth, I'll be sure to let you know.'

'Cheers Mills. Appreciate that.'

'Hey, nice job on the uniform by the way. You can sew, after all! It looks good as –'

'Don't say *good as new*! It never was. Never will be.'

'Fair point.'

R–ing! Ri–! R–! Time for the showdown. Have our teachers read the notes we gave them? Will it make any difference? Is my whole life about to collapse, or do I and my family still have a future? We link arms and head to lesson number one.

CHAPTER 48

Mr Figger

R–ing! Ri–! R–! First, it's drama with Mr Figger, and Snoop's already lurking in the corner with his clipboard.

Mr Figger must have been told about Snoop just now, because I've never seen a teacher look so nervous. He fishes a piece of paper from his pocket, as though he's trying to learn it off by heart. Milly and I clasp each other. That's our note! He thinks it's written by Miss Skipper, and he's going to do what it says!

'I wish he'd stop flashing it around,' says Milly. 'What if Snoop notices?'

'Notices what?' interrupts Trixie, leaning towards us.

Milly groans with exasperation. 'For the last time, Meddle-Minx, stay out of it!'

Trixie smirks and leans even closer. 'Is that one of the notes you passed to the teachers? Something to do with Snoop's inspection? I do hope you're not cheating, ladies. Because that's a serious crime, y'know. Scarecrow Skipper would not be pleased.'

Damn! Trixie's even closer to finding out the truth. But there's no time to answer back: Mr Figger's clapping his hands to start the class. 'Morning, all! Today, we're going to learn the joy of… errr…' He consults his note and finishes the sentence: 'The joy of improvisation!'

'What's improvisation, Sir?' ask several kids, keen and curious. Mr Figger looks desperately at his note. 'Good question. It's umm… errr…'

Damn! We forgot to explain what it means. Snoop leans forward, waiting for Mr Figger's answer. I put up my hand and Mr Figger looks hopeful. 'Yes, Kayla?'

'Sir, does it mean you make it up as you go along?'

'Probably, Kayla. That sounds about right.' He glances at his note again. 'Let's start by bringing a well-known character to life: the Fairy Godmother from Cinderella. OK folks, who wants to go first?'

Several hands shoot up, but Snoop butts in. 'Why don't *you* lead the way, Mr Figger? We'd all benefit from seeing such a talented actor at work. And no doubt you'll enjoy making it up as you go along.' My heart sinks. We're only five minutes into the lesson and it's already failing.

But Mr Figger doesn't know when he's beaten. 'Y– yes of course, Inspector,' he stutters. 'Just give me a moment to create my costume. I ought to look the part, y'know.' He goes over to the cupboard and quickly puts on his outfit:

* A skirt wrapped over his trousers.
* Some high-heeled shoes.
* A ladies' wig.
* Some bright pink lipstick.

Trixie calls out: 'Fairy Godmother? More like something the cat's dragged in!' The Minx Mob guffaw and the rest of the class titters. Milly covers her eyes but peeps through the gap in-between her fingers.

Mr Figger totters into the spotlight – now clutching the cardboard tube from inside a toilet roll, and waving it around wildly. 'Is that meant to be a wand?'

jeers Trixie. 'Looks like he's swatting a fly!' The laughter explodes, and Mr Figger freezes.

'Why doesn't he just get on with it?' grumbles Milly.

'I think it's called stage fright,' I groan, wondering how things can possibly get any worse.

As it turns out, there *is* something worse: Mr Figger's acting. He tries to speak in a lady's voice, but it comes out as a hideous shriek. 'Cinderella, you *shall* go to the wall!'

'Ball, you moron!' shouts Trixie.

'That's what I said!' he protests.

'Oh no you didn't!' shouts Milly.

'Oh yes I did!' he shouts back.

'Oh no you DIDN'T!' shouts the whole class, getting into the pantomime spirit. Clever Milly! Has she actually rescued the situation?

No, because Mr Figger's clearly never been to a pantomime in his life. 'How dare you keep contradicting me?' he yells at the class. 'I've never been so insulted!' He even messes up his exit: the wig falls over his eyes and he trips over his high heels, landing at Snoop's feet.

Trixie calls out: 'You're meant to take a bow, Figger my friend; not a tumble!' The Minx Mob cheer and whistle.

Mr Figger pleads directly with Snoop: 'I do have other skills, Inspector. I'm good at maths, for instance. It's just the drama side that trips me up.'

Snoop's only answer is to scribble away on his clipboard.

For the rest of the lesson, we all take it in turns to improvise the other characters listed in our note. Milly's especially good as Rapunzel. But Mr Figger ruins it by deciding to act the part of her hairbrush, poking out his fingers as the bristles. The only person who enjoys his performance is Trixie. The worse he is, the more she gloats.

As I leave the room at the end of the lesson, I sneak a look at Snoop's clipboard. The page is covered with fierce red crosses. And at the bottom, in big red letters, he's written: 'Mr Figger – drama – FAIL'.

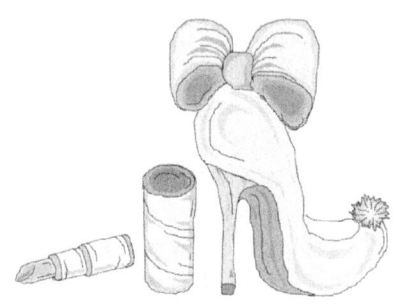

CHAPTER 49

Mr Props

R–ing! Ri–! R–! Next it's maths with Mr Props.

Milly and I are still reeling from this morning's drama lesson, but we tell ourselves that the only way is up. At least with maths, there won't be any wigs or lipstick. Snoop's lurking in the corner again, but Mr Props is busy reading our note and seems to be memorising it, line by line.

'What did you write in it?' Milly asks me hopefully.

'A list of sums.'

'But –'

'Don't worry: I've chosen 'em specially, so they don't use any 6s or 9s.'

'Nice!'

'Yeah, now he'll look like a proper maths teacher.'

Trixie appears out of nowhere. 'Nice try, losers, but you're overruled. I've asked Snoop to give him a 6-and-9 test.'

Milly glares at her. 'D'you actually want Mr Props to fail? In what sick world is that a good idea?'

'Ooh!' smirks Trixie. 'Wouldn't you love to know? Maybe I have secrets too!'

We're desperate to find out more, but we're out of time: Mr Props is starting the lesson. 'Mental arithmetic!' he begins in his big theatrical voice. 'The ability to work out numbers in our head. No calculators needed! Here's a wonderful list of sums for us to try. Who wants to start?'

Snoop speaks up from his corner. 'Might I suggest that we start with a little sum for *you*, Mr Props? We'd all love to see your maths-wizard brain in action.'

Mr Props goes very red. 'Happy to help, Inspector, so long as I tackle one of the sums from my list.'

Snoop loses patience. 'Come along Mr Props, let's not keep the class waiting any longer. What's 69.6 multiplied by 96.9?'

Oh no! He's setting the 6-and-9 sums, just like Trixie asked him to. Mr Props puts his marker pen to the whiteboard, in a desperate bid to write down the sum and work out the answer. But he goes blank and can't even move. SQUEAK! The pen scrapes across the whiteboard, leaving a single wonky line.

'Very well,' sighs Snoop. 'Let's try an easier one. What's 96 divided by 69?'

SQUEAK! Mr Props scrapes out another wonky line, then freezes again. That sends Snoop over the edge. 'Mr Props!' he bellows. 'Please put that pen down and answer a simple question. What's 9 minus 6?' Mr Props stares blankly, opening and closing his mouth, like a fish that's jumped out of its bowl.

'Oh for goodness' sake,' snarls Snoop. 'How about 6 plus 9? I'll give you a clue, Mr Props: the answer lies somewhere between 14 and 16. Any ideas? Any thoughts at all?'

Mr Props falls to his knees and raises his hands towards Snoop, in a big showy gesture that fills the room. 'Could we perhaps try a drama lesson, instead? I used to be a professional actor. The magic of theatre lies at my fingertips, and I'd love to share it with you and the class.'

'Drama, Mr Props?' splutters Snoop. *'Drama?* I don't care if you've played Widow Twanky at the London Palladium. You're here to teach maths!'

Mr Props collapses into a chair, a broken man.

'Class dismissed!' growls Snoop, shooing us away. On the way out, I peep at his red-pen summary, already knowing what it's going to say: 'Mr Props – Maths – FAIL'.

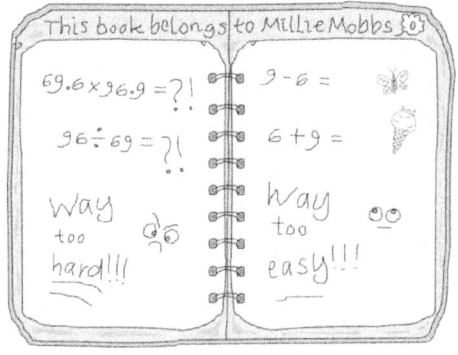

CHAPTER 50

Mrs Choon

R–ing! Ri–! R–! Lunchtime's over, and we're about to start English Language with Mrs Choon.

'Can't be any worse than this morning,' sighs Milly.

'I'm not so sure, Mills. I've got a sinking feeling.'

'Maybe it's that rose petal you ate for breakfast?'

'Oh my god! Am I foaming at the mouth?'

'Nope.'

'My bad feeling's about Trixie. She wants us to fail.'

'Yeah, she wants to bring Clods down. But why?'

'Wish I knew. Whatever's driving her, it's strong.'

We turn to watch her whispering to Snoop in the corner, before slinking to the back of the class.

'Good afternoon!' begins Mrs Choon, clutching the note that we dropped into her bag. 'Today's session is about spelling – a bedrock of our glorious English Language! I'm sure you can't wait to tackle the words on my list. Shall we dive in?'

At first it goes OK. Milly and I get top marks because we know which words are coming up. We can even spell the trickiest ones:

Thingummyjig.

Gobbledegook.

Diarrhoea.

This earns us a round of applause, which makes me squirm because we're cheating. But Milly soaks up the praise, even blowing kisses to her new admirers.

'Wow!' she grins. 'So that's what it feels like to be top of the class! Shame it's taken me twelve years to find out.'

But then it goes wrong. Horribly wrong. And all because Snoop's been tipped off by Trixie.

'Perhaps *I* could suggest the next set of words, Mrs Choon?' he asks, leaning forward.

'Yes of course,' she answers. 'I'm sure that the class will do their best to spell anything you suggest.'

'You misunderstand me, Mrs Choon. I'd like these next words to be spelt by *you*. What a chance for you to show off your familiarity with the dictionary!' That sarcasm means only one thing: he's guessed that she's a truly terrible teacher.

'Really? M- must I?' she stammers.

'Yes Mrs Choon, I'm afraid so.'

'Couldn't I do something musical instead?' she begs. 'I can play any number of songs on the piano, and –'

'Mrs Choon, I need hardly remind you that this is an English Language lesson, not a silly singalong.'

'Very well, Inspector. If you insist.' She stumbles to the whiteboard, picks up a marker pen with trembling fingers, and awaits his suggestions. It soon gets ugly:

* He says *ceiling*.
  She writes *seeling*.
* He says *coffee and sugar*.
  She writes *kofy and shuga*.
* He says *excellent English Language teacher*.
  She writes *egsilant inglish langwij teechur*.

Milly groans like she's got toothache, and pulls her jumper over her face. 'Don't do that,' gloats Trixie. 'You'll miss the fun.'

I punish myself by glancing at Snoop's clipboard on my way out. It says: 'Mrs Choon – English Language – FAIL'.

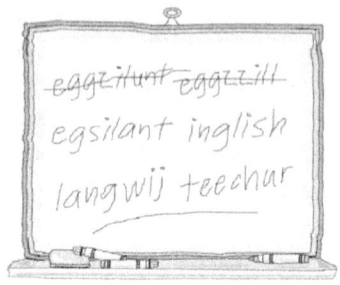

CHAPTER 51

Miss Wurdy

R–ing! Ri–! R–! Our last lesson of the day: music with Miss Wurdy.

She starts by telling us all about the guitar – which is exactly what I suggested in her note. If she talks about music, she's almost OK. It's only when she actually sings or plays anything, that you wish your ears would drop off.

But once again, Trixie out-tricks us. She whispers in Snoop's ear and he asks the dreaded question: 'Why don't you actually play your guitar, Miss Wurdy? It's been hanging round your neck since this lesson began. Or is it simply a fashion accessory?'

'Oh dear,' she squirms. 'This guitar is indeed a musical instrument, but I'm afraid it's missing most of its strings. Perhaps we could do some English Language instead? I'm much better at that.'

'I beg your pardon?'

'English Language. You know: grammar and spelling and the meaning of words.'

'Miss Wurdy, I understand English Language perfectly well. I just fail to grasp its relevance to a music lesson. This *is* meant to be a music lesson, is it not?'

'Yes, Inspector.'

'Then kindly oblige me by playing some actual music!'

'Very well, Inspector.' She carefully tunes her one guitar string and does a lot of coughing. Milly whispers something that sounds like 'Please don't play. Please don't sing. Especially not anything from *Titanic*.'

'And especially not the theme tune,' I think. 'You tried it once before, Miss Wurdy, and we've never quite recovered.'

Miss Wurdy launches in, strumming away and singing at the top of her voice. Yes, it's the *Titanic* theme tune: every verse and chorus. But it's barely a tune at all; imagine a concrete mixer linked to an amplifier, and you're halfway there.

Milly and I try to help by singing along, but we get confused and end up singing different bits at the same time. Trixie and the Minx Mob decide to make it even worse by singing the *Grease* theme tune over the top. A few of the kids put their hands over their ears. They're the musical ones.

When the racket finally stops, Snoop breaks the silence. 'Miss Wurdy,' he sneers. 'We can at least be grateful that you never performed on the actual Titanic.'

'Why's that, Inspector?'

'Because long before the iceberg appeared, every passenger would've hurled themselves into the water!'

'Ouch!' winces Milly.

'But well deserved, don't you think?' cackles Trixie from behind.

Snoop scribbles away on his clipboard. Even though I can't see it, I know what it says: 'Miss Wurdy – Music – FAIL'.

CHAPTER 52

Crunch Time

R–ing! Ri–! R–! Everyone's heading home for the weekend, but Milly and I slump on a bench at the side of the playground.

'Did today really happen?' she begins quietly.

'Oh, it was real, all right.'

'So unfair!'

'Yeah. All our hard work. All those risks. And all for nothing.'

'But Kayla, here's the weird thing: Poop-Snoop *enjoyed* making our teachers look rubbish. Like he wanted 'em to fail. And Trixie's on his side.'

'Yeah, she wants Clods to fail, too. And we still don't know why.'

We watch her head out of the school gates, handing out yet more bags of crisps to the Minx Mob. They scoff them down, then clear off.

'So what happens now?' asks Milly. 'Will Poop-Snoop really close us down?'

'Guess so. That's what it said in Miss Skipper's letter.'

'In that case, I dunno what to say. Apart from *toffee crunch*.'

That's one of her all-time favourite sweets, and she often keeps them with her, in case of emergency. She pulls out a whole bagful now, and for a while we pass it between us, chomping thoughtfully.

The sugar must be working its way into her system, because she begins to sound more hopeful. 'Y'know what, Kayla? Maybe Swindel won't be so bad, once we're all there.'

'Me and my parents will never be there, Mills. The Grimbag hates us.'

'Oh yeah, I forgot. What will you do?'

'Dunno. No school for me. No jobs for Mum and Dad. And if we have to move, no help for Granny.'

Her only answer is to plonk the toffee crunch bag into my lap.

'You sure?' I ask her. 'It's still half full, and I know how much they mean to you.'

'Kayla, right now you need 'em even more than I do. Have as many as you like. And if you need a top-up over the weekend, I can bring some over.' She squeezes my hand then trudges off home.

I should be heading home too, but I'm too depressed to move.

Am I really the same Kayla who used to go to Peach Primary and win awards? Just a few months ago, I was happily messing about with glitter guns and bouncing on trampolines. Now I've lied to my parents, become a criminal, been picked on by the class bully, and dragged my bestie down with me.

'Good afternoon, Inspector. Do come in. I trust you've had a rewarding day. Shall we have some fresh air?' That's Miss Skipper's voice! But where's it coming from? Of course: I'm sitting right outside her office, and she's just opened the window above my head!

'Good afternoon,' replies Snoop. 'Yes, a most rewarding day.'

'Really?' she exclaims, astonished.

'Yes indeed. In fact, it's the best day of my career.'

'So we passed your inspection? Good heavens! I mean, thank goodness! I must confess, that's a huge weight off my mind.'

'Miss Skipper, I –'

'Cup of tea?' she interrupts brightly. 'What better way to toast our success?' I hear her switch on the kettle and get the mugs out of the cupboard.

'Miss Skipper,' he replies. 'You mistake my meaning. My day was rewarding because I'm in a position to alert the authorities to the true state of Clods.'

'Which is -?'

'The four teachers I saw today are the worst I've ever come across. I can only assume that the others are just as shameful.'

CRASH! That's the sound of breaking crockery. Miss Skipper must have dropped the mugs. Snoop ignores the upset and carries on. 'You know what I find most troubling of all? Each of your teachers claimed to be better at a different subject. They even asked me if they could teach that instead!'

'I- I see,' she stammers. 'In that case, I should try and explain –'

'Too late for explanations, Miss Skipper. I've already made my decision.'

I hear his footsteps pace around the room, as he continues in a cold, steady voice. 'I'm giving you one more week to try and fix matters. I shall return next Friday for a final inspection, which you will certainly fail. I shall then summon the local journalists and announce that Clods is being taken over by Swindel.'

Miss Skipper's too shocked to speak, because the only sound is the kettle boiling and switching itself off.

Finally she stammers: 'Cl- Clods will be taken over by... Swindel?'

'Yes, Miss Skipper.'

'And be run by... Gabby Grimm?'

'Indeed. She can't wait to begin.'

'So constant exams? And heartless teachers? And miserable pupils? And –'

'I'm so glad you understand me, Miss Skipper. Yes, Mrs Grimm will replace your teachers with hers. She'll also get rid of most of your pupils, as they'll take too long to reach the required standard. She might keep a handful of your high-performers to boost the exam results. But everyone else must go. That's the positive step your school needs, I'm sure you agree?'

Now Miss Skipper sounds strong and angry. 'No, Inspector, I don't agree! Gabby Grimm's approach isn't the answer and I won't let it happen! I'm the first to admit that Clods isn't perfect; there are many things we need to improve. But we deserve the chance to fix things in our own way, and I demand longer than a week!'

'My dear Miss Skipper, you're hardly in a position to demand anything. I'll be back next Friday and that's final.'

'That's not within the rules, Inspector.'

'Perhaps not,' he replies smoothly. 'But you broke the rules when you gave your teachers those secret notes.'

'I'm sorry?' she croaks.

'The secret notes, Miss Skipper. Full of ridiculous hints for how to run their lessons.'

Disaster: he's got hold of the notes written by Milly and me! I can't bear it any longer: I have to see what's going on. I climb up onto the bench and carefully peep through the window.

CHAPTER 53

Snoop vs. Skipper

This is what I see: Snoop's clutching our notes and waving them under Miss Skipper's nose. He's smirking in a way that makes you want to snap his red pen in two, stamp all over his clipboard and twist his tie pin into a mangled mess.

Miss Skipper looks as broken as the mugs that lie in pieces all around her. She's still gripping one of the handles, even though the cup bit has broken off.

'I've never seen these notes before,' she croaks. 'You must believe me.'

'Nice try, Miss Skipper. But they're signed by you.'

'Once again, Inspector: I did not write these notes. Perhaps one of my pupils is playing some kind of joke?'

He laughs scornfully. 'You don't give up, do you? These notes are your shameful attempt to pass my inspection. It's cheating and you know it. If you've any sense, you'll start packing up now.'

'But Inspector - how did these notes reach you?'

'One of your smartest pupils got hold of them and handed them to me.'

'Don't tell me: Trixie Minx.'

'How did you know?'

'Just a guess.'

He strides towards the door, then remembers something and turns round again. 'Oh, and I've told

Gabby Grimm to watch out for two members of your staff. She's promised me that she'll fire them, as soon as she takes over.'

He fishes out his clipboard and reads out the two names that I'm dreading. 'First, your Assistant Caretaker, Mr Grub. He had the nerve to point out that I'd helped myself to your parking space and damaged your *Headteacher* sign. Second, your Chief Washer-Upper, Mrs Grub. At lunchtime, she stopped me taking three extra helpings of custard - simply because it'd leave the others without any. How dare anyone at Clods speak to me like that? Let alone the two people at the bottom of your heap!'

I don't know whether to laugh or cry: Mum and Dad actually stood up to Snoop! I'm proud of them, even though it'll cost them their jobs.

Now Miss Skipper's shaking with anger. 'Inspector Snoop, no one at Clods is bottom of the heap! All my staff are equally valued. Mr and Mrs Grub are wonderful, hard-working people who make a vital contribution to my school. I demand that they keep their jobs!'

'Miss Skipper, can I remind you that you failed today's inspection? Your days of issuing demands are over. In any case, those wretched Grubs deserve to be taught a lesson.'

'How dare you?' She jabs her finger at him, forgetting that she's still clutching the broken mug handle. It comes dangerously close to his face but he doesn't flinch. 'Miss Skipper, you've just tried to attack my face with broken crockery. In my report, I shall inform the authorities that you're violently out of control. I'm sure they'll want to take action against you. And quite right too.'

'But –'

'Now I really must go. May I conclude this delightful conversation by wishing you a pleasant weekend.'

I crouch behind the bench, watching him march back to his car. Once again, he stops to check his appearance in the wing mirror, patting his little moustache and smoothing those greasy strands of hair over the top of his head. Then he zooms off, leaving a thick cloud of fumes hanging in the air.

I peep back at Miss Skipper, who now looks older and dustier than ever. She picks up the pile of notes which Milly and I thought would save her, buries her face in them, and bursts into tears.

I creep away with the sickening knowledge that I've made everything worse. Granny said I'm smart; she said I'll find a way to put things right. But she's wrong: I've blown a massive hole in our lives, and it's so big it'll never be fixed.

Back at home, I'm hiding in my room by the time Mum and Dad get home. Dad calls up the stairs: 'Hey Kukoo, hope you've had a grand old day?' Mum calls out too: 'What d'you fancy for tea, Kukoo? Pancakes or omelette?' I want to tell them that I love them but they'll know something's wrong, because I've barely ever said it before. I wipe away a tear and call out the only thing I can: 'Pancakes please.'

CHAPTER 54

Not Hungry

After just one pancake, I give up and stare into space.
'What's up?' Dad asks me.
'Nothing. Just not hungry.'
He helps himself to my spare pancakes and carries on. 'OK then, here's something that'll make you smile. Guess what happened at school today? Well, one of the visitors parked in Miss Skipper's space and knocked her sign over. When I pointed this out to him, he made a note of my name.'
'I'm not smiling yet, Dad.'
'Wait, there's more. Why d'you think this guy was so interested in me? Surely there's only one reason: he wanted to tell Miss Skipper that I'm doing a great job!'
'Ooh,' says Mum. 'Did he have a little moustache and a tie pin? I met him at lunchtime. I stopped him taking a triple-helping of custard and he was kind enough to write down my name, too. Now it all makes sense.'
'Now what makes sense?' I ask, alarmed.
Mum leans in close, as though sharing a secret. 'Remember those job promotions we talked about?'
'Head Caretaker and Dinner Lady?'
She nods like I've just said 'President and Film Star'. 'Those new jobs are going to be ours, Kukoo! Miss Skipper told us so, herself!'

Hugging each other, they reach out and grip my hands. 'Isn't it amazing, Kukoo? More money and a proper career! All thanks to that funny-looking visitor. He must have persuaded Miss Skipper to give us this chance!'

'When did she tell you about the new jobs?'

'Just after lunch.'

Now it makes sense. When Miss Skipper announced the new jobs, she still hoped that Clods had a future. She never imagined that it would be seized by the Grimbag.

'When do the new jobs start?' I ask them, weakly.

'Next Friday, Kukoo. Just a week away!'

It couldn't be worse: that's the day of Snoop's final visit, when he'll announce that he's closing the whole place down. How can I tell them that they'll be ripped apart? By the man who they think is helping them?

They're waiting for me to say something happy, so I make a massive effort: 'Well that's... just...'

'Brilliant?' suggests Dad.

'The nicest news ever?' suggests Mum.

I manage to nod.

'And the best thing of all?' continues Mum. 'You're doing well too, Kukoo! You're getting the education you need to become a doctor or –'

'Astronaut,' interrupts Dad. 'Yes, Kukoo: you're at the top-class school you deserve. Now if only Granny could get well again, everything would be perfect.'

Mum ruffles my hair. 'Shall we celebrate with a triple-choc pudding? It's your favourite, after all. And as it happens, there's one in the freezer.'

I honestly think it'd choke me. Because all their hopes are going to come crashing down, and there's nothing I can do to stop it.

I get up and shuffle towards the door. 'Actually, I think I'll just go and lie down.'

'Oh darling!' exclaims Mum. 'Are you ill?'

'Not really. Just tired.'

'OK love, forget the pudding. Why don't you have a bubble bath, instead? Once you're done, I'll bring you a hot water bottle and a nice fresh cuppa.'

'Thanks, Mum. That'll be nice.'

Cleo's waiting for me halfway up the stairs, so I sit down next to her and stroke her softly. Mum and Dad don't realise I'm there, because their chatter drifts towards me. 'What's wrong with Kukoo?' begins Dad. 'She doesn't seem very excited about our new jobs.'

'It's her age, Kevin. All those hormones rushing around her body. I was just the same when I was growing up.'

'If you say so. All women are a mystery to me! Poor Kukoo. Hope those hormones don't wreck anything. The rest of her life is going so well.'

That's way more than I want to hear. I creep upstairs to my room and close the door.

I can't help wishing that Mr Bunnyfun was still here. When Milly brought him over, I laughed at her for being so childish. But all I want to do right now is push my face into his big fluffy tummy and cry my eyes out. I bury myself under the duvet and cry my eyes out anyway.

CHAPTER 55

Wet Weekend

The whole of Saturday, I mope around in my bedroom. Granny's having some extra tests done today, so we can't go and see her. And it's raining, so there's no point going out.

Flicking through my notebook, I come across the doodles I drew, just before I went to see Miss Skipper:

Doctor Kayla, saving a patient.
Engineer Kayla, building a mega bridge.
Prime Minister Kayla, leading the country.
Astronaut Kayla, landing on Mars.

I don't believe in any of those Kaylas anymore; they're never going to happen. I rip out the page and tear it to pieces.

Dad pops his head round my door. 'Fancy a treat this evening? It's ages since we had a family outing. Why not invite Milly too? What d'you reckon, Kukoo: cinema? Pizza? Bowling?'

'Not all three, I'm afraid,' adds Mum, peering round his shoulder. 'We can't afford that until we start our new jobs. But one of them's fine. So what's it to be, Kukoo? Your choice.'

'No thanks.'

'You mean you'd like us to choose?'

'No, I just don't feel like going out. Sorry.'

They swap a worried look and creep away, still whispering about my hormones. I bury my head under the pillow, hating myself. I'm a liar and a loser. I've gone and spoilt everything they're proud of. They haven't found out yet, but they soon will.

On Sunday morning I wake up early, and decide to sneak a visit to Granny. Now that everything's gone wrong, I want to ask her what to do. But Mum and Dad hear me getting up and insist on coming too. Granny and I don't get a single moment to ourselves.

The journey home's rubbish too, because our bus breaks down. We set off walking the rest of the way, even though the weather's wetter than a wet sponge.

We're still trudging through the puddles on the high street, when we spot someone curled up in a doorway, huddled inside a sleeping bag. It's pulled right over their head too, as if they can't face the world.

'Shocking!' tuts Mum. 'No one should have to live on the streets, especially in this foul weather.'

Dad goes over to the hunched figure and holds out some coins. 'Sorry it's not more, mate. But maybe you can put it towards a hot meal?'

A voice answers from inside the sleeping bag, and we're shocked that they sound as young as me. In fact, I'm sure I've heard that voice before.

'Thanks,' says the voice. 'That's really kind of you. But I've got lots of money. I'm running away from home, that's all. I've just stopped here for a rest, on my way to London.'

No. Surely it can't be... A head pops out at the top of the bag. Billy!

CHAPTER 56

Runaway Boy

When Billy sees me, he doesn't know whether to laugh or cry. 'Kayla!' he cries out. 'This is the last time we'll meet, so it's hello and goodbye.'

Mum and Dad stare at me in surprise. 'Kukoo, d'you actually know this boy?'

'I'm Billy Mobbs,' he tells them, covering his head with a newspaper to try and keep the rain off.

'Milly's brother!' declares Dad. 'Blimey mate, you're the spitting image!'

Mum bends down and strokes Billy's hair. 'Goodness, sweetheart - you're soaked. We need to get you home before you freeze to death.'

'No way!' he growls through chattering teeth. 'London's the only place for me now.'

'Billy love,' she continues softly. 'I don't know why you're running away, but whatever it is, I'm sure you'd rather talk to your mum and sort it out. She'll be frantic with worry about you.'

'You don't understand!' he protests. 'My mum's not like you. She doesn't care about me at all!'

'I'm sure that's not true,' frowns Mum. 'Maybe she's just got a different way of showing it.'

'Huh!' he scoffs. 'Well in that case, why won't she let me leave Swindel, even though it's killing me?'

185

Close to tears, he hides his face in the wet newspaper. 'Tell 'em, Kayla! Make 'em listen!'

I open my mouth, even though I don't know what I'm going to say. 'Billy, I –'

RING RING! Billy's mobile goes off. It's Milly, so he puts her on speaker-phone. 'Finally!' she shrieks. 'Why didn't you answer, before? I've been searching everywhere. You're scaring me, Bruv. Where the hell are you?'

'In a soggy sleeping bag.'

'What?! Where?'

'In the doorway of a shop on the high street.'

'I suppose this is your latest protest?'

'Sort of.'

'Well stay right there, cos I'm coming to get you. I'll call a cab and be there before you know it. Then I'm bringing you straight home – so there!' She rings off before he can argue back.

'Don't even think about running off!' Mum warns him. 'We're staying right here with you until your sister arrives.'

To prove the point, she coaxes him out of his sleeping bag and wraps him in her own coat. Dad and I put our own coats round him too, but it's still not enough to stop him shivering. So I run to the Hug-a-Mug café to buy a hot cup of soup, and press it into his hands.

As he sips the soup, he gives us all a strange look. 'Don't suppose Milly and I could come and live with you lot? We won't be any trouble, y'know. We'll help with the hoovering and sleep in the shed.'

'You know that's not possible,' Mum tells him gently.

'It is!' he insists. 'We'll hoover as often as you like. And if your shed's too small, we'll buy you a bigger one.'

'No, I mean that you and Milly belong with your own mum. She does love you, Billy – even if you don't see it.'

He scowls into his cup. 'You're so nice, you think everyone else is, too.'

Milly's cab arrives. I don't know whether she's more upset about Billy, or more surprised to see that he's being looked after by the Grubs.

The cab's one of those minibus ones, so Milly and Billy insist that we climb in, too. Our wet clothes turn the cab floor into a puddle, but the driver stops grumbling about it when Milly promises him a big tip. They drop us off at our house, waving goodbye through the steamed-up window.

Later that evening, I call Milly. 'How's Billy doing?'

'Coughing and sneezing all over the place. Remind me never to sleep in a soggy sleeping bag.'

'What about your mum? Don't suppose she's letting him switch to Clods?'

'As if! She's still ignoring him.'

'Next time, he'll do something even more stupid.'

'I know. It's unbearable!'

'Can I tell you something bad, too?'

'Go on.'

'Snoop's coming back this Friday.'

'That soon? How d'you know?'

'After you'd gone home, I heard him telling Miss Skipper. Next Friday, he's gonna close us down.'

She lets out a long, low groan.

'There's more, Mills. Trixie got hold of our teachers' notes. She handed 'em to Snoop, and he's shown 'em to Miss Skipper.'

'Oh my god! What did she say?'

'She told him she'd never seen the notes before, but he didn't believe her.'

'Damn, damn, damn!'

'And we still don't know why Trixie's mixed up in all this.'

'My head's swimming.'

'Mine too. See you tomorrow, Mills.'

'Night, Kayla.'

When I go to bed, I find the rest of the toffee crunch that Milly gave me on Friday. It's covered in fluff from my schoolbag but I eat it anyway, hoping it'll make things seem normal again. Cleo paws at me to go and brush my teeth, but I can't be bothered.

I fall asleep with my teeth stuck together, dreaming that the world's spinning out of control.

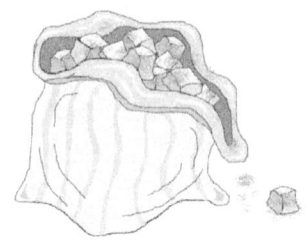

CHAPTER 57

Grimm View

At school the next morning, I find a heartbroken Milly peering through the railings into the Swindel playground. Billy's standing in the usual line, but he looks as sick as Cleo, that time she broke into a nearby house and ate a bowl of dogfood.

'Look at him, Kayla: he should be in bed, not at school.'

'Yeah, and especially not at Swindel!'

'That's just what I told Mum, but would she listen? She says it's his own fault for protesting in a soggy sleeping bag. Plus he's got five exams today, so she told him to stop sniveling and get on with it.'

The kids shout out their school motto but Billy just sneezes: 'All Work, No... ACHOO!' The sneeze is too much for the whistle-blowing teacher: he marches over to Billy and hands him a slip of paper, coloured in the Swindel purple and gold.

'Hey Mills, what's that?'

'Billy's told me about it. It says *Work Beats Food*.'

'Meaning?'

'Instead of eating anything this lunchtime, he'll have to sit an extra exam. I can't bear it!'

Billy's had enough, too: he defiantly stuffs the slip of paper into his mouth, gives it a big chew, and swallows it down. That makes the teacher go red with fury: he hands Billy two more purple-and-gold papers, and marches him inside.

'Oh it's too much!' wails Milly.

As the door slams on Billy, we realise that the Grimbag's seen the whole thing. She's at her usual window, hovering over the playground like a hawk. Her fierce dark eyebrows are frowning with disapproval, scrunched together in the middle of her forehead. Then she's joined by someone else, and her frown gives way to flashy smiles.

As this other person steps forward, we see that it's a man. A man with a little moustache, a long nose, and a tie pin that glints in the sunlight. 'Poop-Snoop!' exclaims Milly. 'Trust him to turn up next door!'

'And look, Mills: they're laughing together! As though they're friends!'

She's about to reply, when Miss Skipper appears at the Clods main door and shouts: 'Kayla Grub. My office. NOW!' The whole playground goes quiet: everyone stops what they're doing and stares at me, wondering what I've done to make Miss Skipper so angry.

Milly takes my arm. 'No way you're facing this alone, Kayla. I'm coming too.' But Miss Skipper shouts 'Kayla only, please!' and Milly has to let me go.

I weave my way through the gawping crowd and follow Miss Skipper into her office. It feels like the longest walk of my life. My legs have turned to jelly, my tummy's churning away, and I wonder if I'm going to be sick.

I'm about to face up to all my Clods crimes.

CHAPTER 58

Detective Skipper

When I follow Miss Skipper into her office, the first thing I notice is her empty vase. Without those yellow roses, the room seems dark and gloomy.

'Yes, it's a shame isn't it?' she begins. 'Someone chose to destroy the beautiful rosebush outside the staffroom. What kind of person would do such a thing? Actually, don't answer that; I didn't summon you here to talk about flowers.'

She thrusts a pile of papers towards me. It's the twelve teachers' notes. 'Well, Kayla, I expect you recognise your handiwork. Please don't try to deny it. You're the only person who I told about Inspector Snoop's visit. This was your foolish attempt to help my teachers pass the inspection.'

'I'm so sorry, Miss. I was only trying to help.'

'Well, I'm afraid you've gone and made things a whole lot worse. What on earth were you thinking of?'

I think it's the sort of question I'm not meant to answer, so I keep quiet. She walks over to me, now brittle and tight-lipped. 'Kayla Grub, please show me your sleeves.' I know what's coming. I unroll my sleeves and hold them out towards her, so she can inspect the big rip that I mended.

'I congratulate you on the quality of your sewing. But it's as I suspected: you set off the fire alarm. How do I know? Because your father showed me a thread of Clods jumper that had caught on the smashed glass.'

'Yes Miss: that thread was mine, and now it's back in my jumper. But my parents don't know.'

'I see.'

'My dad brought the thread home, but now he thinks that my cat ate it.'

She puts her hand to her forehead. 'Kayla, I'm appalled that you've lied to your parents, on top of everything else. But can we please put your cat to one side for the moment?'

'That's actually quite hard in real life, Miss. Cos if anyone tries to shove her to one side, she comes straight back at you. I've often wondered if –'

'Enough!'

'Yes Miss. Sorry Miss. No more cat.'

'To return to the topic in hand: why did you set off the fire alarm? I already know the answer: it was the only way to get your notes into the teachers' bags. Am I correct?'

'Yes Miss.'

'Tell me: was anyone else involved?'

'No, Miss. Just me, Miss.' Another lie. But I can't get Milly into trouble; she helped me because I begged her.

'Well thank heavens you didn't drag anyone else into this mess. I'm grateful for that, at least. As you may appreciate, I've got far more important things to worry about.'

'What sort of things, Miss?' As soon as I've said it I know I've gone too far. She half-stumbles backwards, to lean against her desk. 'For goodness' sake Kayla, do you really think I'm going to tell you? I made that mistake when you last came to see me, and look where that led! No, this time I'll keep my problems to myself, thank you very much.' She stares at the empty vase, lost in thought.

I can guess what's bugging her. Snoop's back this Friday for his final inspection, then he'll hand Clods to the Grimbag. Plus he'll tell Head Office that she attacked him with broken crockery. No wonder she's on edge.

I'm scared to break the silence, but there's one more thing I need to ask. 'Miss Skipper?'

'Yes, Kayla?'

'Please can you not tell my parents that I'm in trouble? It'd break their hearts. They wanted me to be Prime Minister, y'see. Or an astronaut. Or –' I tail off because it sounds ridiculous.

Does she smile a tiny little bit, or do I just imagine it? 'Kayla, I accept that you meant well and that you're genuinely sorry. I can confirm that I won't be involving your parents at this point.'

'Thank you, Miss. Shall I go now, Miss?'

'Not so fast, young lady. Don't think for one moment that you're getting away with it. I'm going to give you the worst punishment I can think of.'

My mind goes into panic overdrive. What if the punishment's something to do with those stinky underpants from the lost property cupboard? What if she makes me carry them around, trying to find out who they belong to? I'd rather die.

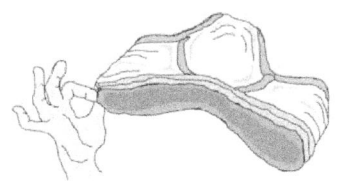

'Please listen carefully, Kayla. Miss Hillock's last games lesson ended rather badly when the tug-of-war team and the hula-hoop team got tangled up with each other. Your ever-helpful father had to go and pull everyone out. The ropes and the hula-hoops are still lying in a knotted heap in the changing rooms.'

'Sorry to hear that, Miss. But what's that got to do with the punishment?'

'Your task is to untangle the mess. And you'll do it this lunchtime, so the equipment is ready for Miss Hillock's class this afternoon. Do I make myself clear?'

'Yes Miss. I'll sort it. Promise.' So that's Miss Skipper's worst punishment? It sounds a doddle. What gets me is that I've let her down so badly. I can see the disappointment in her eyes, and it twists inside me like a knife.

I'm halfway out of the door, when she calls me back. 'One more thing, Kayla: you'll be sharing the punishment with Trixie Minx.'

'Trixie, Miss?'

'Yes, Kayla. I only discovered your notes because Trixie passed them to Inspector Snoop. She knows full well that she should have brought them straight to me. So in my mind, she's equally to blame.'

'But I was trying to save the school! Trixie's trying to destroy it!'

'Don't answer back, Kayla. You're in enough trouble already. You and Trixie will share the punishment and that's my final word on the matter. Now get along with you.'

'Yes Miss.'

CHAPTER 59

Unpicking It

R–ing! Ri–! R–! It's lunchtime and I'm in the changing room, staring at a rope-and-hula-hoop mountain that's piled halfway to the ceiling. This job's way bigger than I thought.

I try unpicking some of the knots, but they're so tight I can't wiggle them free. What am I going to do? I promised Miss Skipper that I'd finish the whole lot in my lunchbreak. And where the hell is Trixie? She's meant to be here too.

She turns up five minutes late and flops down in the corner. 'Hurry up, Frizz-Face, or we'll be here all day!'

Those frowning dark eyebrows remind me of someone, but who? Is it someone I've seen recently, or is my mind playing tricks on me?

'Looking forward to Snoop's next visit?' says Trixie, determined to pick a fight. But this time I keep calm. 'Why d'you want Clods to fail?' I ask her, simply.

'Cos it's filled with losers like you.'

'Come on, Trixie; you don't really mean it – not deep-down. OK, the teachers are rubbish, but maybe Miss Skipper can fix that somehow. And everyone's nice and friendly. Well, everyone except you and the Minx Mob.'

I'm expecting her to bite back again, but this time, all she does is bite her lip. 'What's up?' I ask her.

'You think it's easy, being Trixie Minx?' she blurts out, furiously wiping a tear from her cheek.

'Yes, actually. Your life's way easier than mine. Loads of kids look up to you. You've got smooth, swishy hair. Your school uniform fits properly. You talk like everyone else around here; you don't sound different. What more d'you need?'

She wipes away another tear. 'Huh! If only you knew…'

I go back to wrestling with my knot. Maybe if I keep quiet she'll tell me her secret. And it works! She starts to open up, in a softer voice that I've never heard before. 'I'm not who you think I am.'

'Who are you then, Trixie? I'm listening.'

She takes a deep breath, but just as she's about to speak, the Minx Mob crash into the room:

> 'Found you at last, boss! We've been looking everywhere!'
>
> 'Hey boss, why are you hanging out with Frizz Face?'
>
> 'Aren't you always telling us she looks like a dustbin?'

In a flash, Trixie turns back to her old self. 'A dustbin?' she sneers. 'Look at her: she's a whole rubbish tip! Would you be seen dead in that mouldy old uniform? And what about that weirdo accent? It's freak-speak!' The Minx Mob burst out laughing and Trixie flounces off with them, swishing her pony-tail as if our other chat never happened.

Damn! I was so close to finding out the real Trixie. When will I ever get that chance again? And I still haven't freed a single hula-hoop. I have another go at an easy-looking knot that's falling open, but all I do is make it tighter. Cursing bitterly, I throw it back onto the pile.

'Need any help?' says a friendly voice from the doorway.

'Mills! Am I glad to see you! These flippin' knots won't budge.'

She turns out to be a knot-busting superhero: her fingers fly along like magic. Every time she frees a hula-hoop, I stack it neatly in the corner. And while we work, I tell her about this morning's meeting with Miss Skipper.

'How come she didn't send for me, too?' asks Milly.

'I kept your name out of it. She thinks I acted alone.'

She flushes with pained gratitude. 'Won't that make things worse for you?'

'Only if she finds out about the cover-up. In any case, she's much more worried about Snoop's visit this Friday.'

'Yeah, the final showdown. Still can't believe it, Kayla. And there's nothing more we can do.'

As her magic fingers work through the knots, an idea suddenly clicks in my brain. I pace around the room, seized with wild energy.

'You're trampling on the ropes!' grumbles Milly.

I should stop and apologise, but I'm too fired up. 'What if we could get to the bottom of it, Mills? Solve the mystery? Crack the code?'

'Hello? What are you actually talking about?'

'Here's what's bugged me, right from the start: all of our teachers are really good at something. It's just not the subject they actually teach.'

'True. Nothing new, there.'

'But here's the thing: it's like they're all MIXED UP IN EACH OTHER'S JOBS!'

She pauses in the middle of a knot. 'Hmm. Hadn't thought of it like that.'

I pace around even faster. 'So why can't they all just SWAP OVER?'

'You mean swap to the subject they're good at?'

'Exactly!' I exclaim, practically running around the room. 'So Mr Figger would teach maths. And Miss Zinc would teach science. And... WAAAH!' I trip over a rope and crash onto the hula-hoops.

'Y'know what?' she smiles. 'I think you're onto something.'

'What am I onto, Mills? An idea? Or just a pile of games equipment?'

'Ha ha. Very funny. An idea, of course.' I wait for her to add that I'm a genius, but instead she says 'Oops. Problem.'

'Go on.'

'If it was easy to swap the teachers over, why didn't Miss Skipper do it years ago?'

'Cos something's stopping her. Whatever it is, I'm gonna find out.'

'She'll never explain it to you, Kayla. You're in trouble, remember?'

'Yeah, but what if I sneak a look around her office? Maybe the answer's in there, somewhere.'

'Are you kidding? What if you're caught? Are you trying to get thrown out of school?'

'What have I got to lose? If the Grimbag takes over Clods, she'll throw me out, anyway. That's why we've gotta go for it!'

'Hang on, did you just say *we*?'

'Yeah. I need your help again, Mills. I can't do this on my own.'

'But –'

'D'you want Clods to go under? D'you want me and my family to be forced out of town? D'you want Granny Grub to be left all alone? D'you want Billy to be stuck with the Grimbag forever?'

She unpicks the last few knots, then storms out of the room. For a terrible moment, I think she's abandoned me – but she rushes back in and grabs my arm. 'Come on, Kayla: I thought you were right behind me! We've still got twenty minutes until our next lesson. Let's go check out that office!'

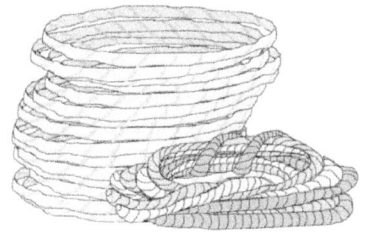

CHAPTER 60

Photo Girls

We're in luck. Miss Skipper has left a scribbled note on her door:

Gone to get library book: 'How to Deal with a Crisis and Still Be a Nice Person'. Back by end of lunchbreak.

Milly's itching to begin. 'Don't worry, Kayla: I'll keep a lookout. If anyone gets too close, I'll give you an owl hoot.'

'Hate to say it, Mills, but I've never seen an owl flying around the Clods corridor. Can't you do a different noise?'

'Y'know what?' she sniffs. 'Sometimes you're way too picky.'

'But this whole school's an owl-free zone. When's the last time one flew over the playground?'

'Fine!' she snaps. 'I'll sing something instead.'

'What tune?'

'Does it matter? Stop dawdling and get in there!' She opens the door and shoves me inside.

Where do I start? I don't even know what I'm looking for; just some sort of clue. Something that explains why our teachers are stuck in each other's jobs, and why they can't swap back again.

I rush around the room, picking things up then putting them down again, no wiser than I started. Oh, this is hopeless, and I'm running out of time.

Hey, one stack of paper looks less dusty than the others. Maybe it was moved recently? I'll take a look.

The papers on top are school dinner menus from years ago: egg and chips, sticky toffee pudding, jam sponge and custard. No clues, there. Underneath, there's a box, labelled in Miss Skipper's handwriting: *Things That Keep Me Going When I Want To Give Up*. Ooh, that sounds better. I open the lid and look inside.

It's full of cards, thanking Miss Skipper for doing all sorts of kind, helpful things. There's even one from Dad:

> *Dear Miss Skipper, thank you for letting Krystal, Kayla and me join Clods. We'll do our best to make you proud.*

If only he'd known how it'd turn out. But I haven't got time to cry; I have to keep going.

At the bottom of the box, there's a photo of two smiling girls in Clods uniform. I can tell the photo's old, because the colours have gone funny, turning the Clods mud-brown into the shade of burnt toast. But this isn't any old photo; it's labelled *Pippa and Gabby Skipper*!

The Pippa girl is Miss Skipper herself. That's the name she used when she first wrote to Mum and Dad about their jobs. In any case, it's Miss Skipper's face. So this photo must be from *centuries* ago.

What about Gabby Skipper, the other girl? She's got glossy black hair and thick dark eyebrows and – oh my god – now I get goosebumps. Because I'm staring at the childhood face of the Grimbag!

Now I recognise her name, too: when Miss Skipper talked to Snoop last Friday, she mentioned the Grimbag's first name, and it was *Gabby*!

What about the surname, though? Well I guess that Gabby Skipper ended up marrying some poor bloke called Grimm, and got the new surname to match. It all adds up.

This one little photo is pure gold. Miss Skipper and the Grimbag are SISTERS! And their school was CLODS!

On the back of the photo, there's a squiggly line in Miss Skipper's handwriting: *When my little sister was still my best friend.* The ink's splashed, as if she's cried on it. I've barely got my head around all of this, when I find something else so crazy, it rewires my whole brain.

It's another photo, half-hidden under a scrap of tissue paper. This one shows the Grimbag as a young woman, holding a baby. But this time, it's the baby that catches my eye, because it's a super-cute version of the Grimbag. It's even got the Grimbag's glossy dark hair and thick dark eyebrows.

My hands suddenly tremble so much, the photo goes blurry. That hair! Those eyebrows! Surely it can't be... I turn the photo over, and even though I'm still shaking, I can read Miss Skipper's message: *My beautiful new niece. Welcome to the world, Trixie!*

Yes, that baby is our very own Trixie Minx! So that's Trixie's secret! The Minx surname is just a cover-up; she's really Trixie Grimm! The Grimbag's her MUM! And Miss Skipper's her AUNTIE!

'Daisy, Daisy, give me your answer, do!'

In the corridor just outside, Milly's belting out a song. I've never heard anyone sing so loudly. Not even Miss Wurdy, our terrible music teacher. Someone must be heading this way!

With lightning speed, I drop the photos back in the box, cover them with the 'thank you' cards, and slam the lid shut. I even remember to stack the school dinner menus back on top. Hopefully Miss Skipper won't spot that anyone's touched it.

'DAISY, DAISY, GIVE ME YOUR –' Milly's now singing so loudly, it's almost a scream. I spring back into the corridor and she pounces on me, pulling me straight round the corner.

'Only just in time, Kayla. Look!' We peer back towards the office and see Miss Skipper disappear inside, clutching a library book.

'Daisy Daisy?' I giggle. 'Isn't that song from – like – pre-history?'

'Guess I panicked. No wonder they all laughed at me.'

'Impressive volume, Mills.'

'Please tell me it was worth it. Did you find anything?'

'Yeah, and you're never gonna believe it.'

'Try me.'

'Miss Skipper and the Grimbag are connected.'

'So?' she shrugs. 'We knew that already. They're both headteachers. Their schools are next door to each other.'

'It's more than that, Mills. They're *sisters*!'

She looks as shocked as though I'd said that they're trained killers. 'No way, Kayla! How d'you know?'

'Cos I found their old school photo, labelled with their names. Oh, and guess which school? I'll give you a clue. It's very close to here.'

'Swindel?'

'Oops. Bad clue. Think even closer, Mills.'

'Clods?'

'You got it!'

She blinks, trying to take it all in.

'There's something else, Mills: a photo that shows something mind-blowing about Trixie.'

'Tell me now, or I'll go mad!'

'She's Miss Skipper's niece – and the Grimbag's daughter!'

I thought she'd explode with excitement, but she shakes her head. 'Sorry Kayla, but you're wrong there. Trixie's a Minx, remember? Not a Grimm.'

'That surname's false. Made up. Totally pretend.'

She blinks, startled all over again. 'Why would Trixie do that?'

'Would *you* want anyone to know that the Grimbag was your mum?'

'Fair point. And now you come to mention it, Trixie does look like the Grimbag. Just the pretty version.'

She finally gives me the admiring glance I'm so desperate for. 'It's gobsmacking, Kayla. Is this gonna stop Poop-Snoop? And save Clods?'

Damn! I'd forgotten that bit. I give an awkward shrug, and now she tuts with disapproval. 'Kayla, you need to hurry up and think of something. Poop-Snoop's coming back just three days' time.'

'Thanks for reminding me. Any ideas, yourself?'
'No, but I'll tell you who can help.'
'Who?'
'Granny Grub. You're always telling me she's the smartest person you know.'

Why didn't I think of that? I'll go and see her, straight after school.

R–ing! Ri–! R–! We head to the afternoon's lessons feeling a bit more positive.

CHAPTER 61

Granny's Guess

It's only one day since I last saw Granny, but she seems a whole century older. When she tries to squeeze my hand I can barely feel it. Her head doesn't leave the pillow and her eyes have lost their twinkle. What's the point of Granny being in hospital if they can't make her better? I glare at the nurses but they're too busy rushing around to notice.

At least she can still speak, even if it's only a tiny croak. 'Well, Kayla sweetheart: did you write the notes for the teachers?' It's her first chance to ask me, because for once Mum and Dad aren't hanging around.

'Yes, Granny. I guessed that's what your story was telling me to do. But it didn't work. Cos I messed up.' To avoid looking her in the eye, I fiddle with one of the tubes that's sticking out of her arm.

'Don't be too hard on yourself, love. I'm sure you did your best.'

'But Granny, it's worse than that! Snoop's coming back this Friday and he's gonna hand Clods over to the Grimbag.'

'The what-bag?'

'She's the toxic nightmare who runs the school next door. She's the one who spat me out when Dad first wrote to her. So she'll throw me out again, and I'll be left with no school at all. I'll grow up never understanding geometry or knowing the capital of Brussels!'

'Brussels *is* a capital, darling. The capital of Belgium.'

'There you go! My point exactly. She's planning to throw out Mum and Dad, too – just cos they stood up to Snoop. Who else will take 'em on, around here? What if we have to leave town? Who'll look after you then? It's all my fault, Granny! I'm one stupid massive failure!'

I pour out the whole story: my teachers being mixed up in each other's jobs; the Grimbag, Miss Skipper and Trixie being related; everyone being tangled up in this big mess, with the winners taking everything and the losers left with nothing.

Granny listens carefully and manages to put her arm round me, but this makes the tubes tug at her skin and now I feel guilty as hell. I wipe my tears on her hospital blanket and try to look fine. She waits for me to calm down, then gives me her advice. 'If you ask me, it sounds like the Grimbag and Snoop are hiding something.'

'Really, Granny? Hiding what, though?'

'That's for you to find out. I think it's the clue to this whole puzzle.'

'What about Trixie? Why's she trying to wreck Clods, too?'

'What if her mum sent her to Clods to cause trouble? Deep down, Trixie hates the role she's been forced into. But she knows it's the only way to please her mum. No matter how horrible her mum is, Trixie's still desperate to gain her love.'

'Blimey, Granny. How d'you know all this?'

'Oh, it's just a hunch. I've been around a long time, y'know.'

'OK, so how do I find what the Grimbag and Snoop are hiding?'

'Well you seem to be good at sneaking into places. Why not try the Grimbag's office?'

'But Swindel isn't even my school!'

'D'you remember the saying I wrote in that little card I sent you, just before you left Olding?'

I screw up my eyes to try and remember. 'I've got it, Granny! *Every door has its own key.*'

'That's right, sweetheart. And I said that you'll always find the key if you look hard enough. Never forget how smart and brave you are, Kayla.'

'Huh! I feel about as smart and brave as a plank of wood.'

'Oh you'll find a way, darling. I know you will.'

I'm about to leave, when I remember that Granny has two secrets of her own: the note and necklace, hidden in her wardrobe. Maybe if I ask in the right way, she won't mind explaining them.

'Granny, can I ask you something else?'

'Of course, love. Anything you like.'

'Well, you know your wardrobe –'

BEEP BEEP!!! The machine at the top of her bed flashes a warning. A nurse rushes up to check one of her tubes (the one I fiddled with) and bundles me out of the way. Time for me to go.

Just before I leave the ward, I turn back and wave. 'Thanks, Granny. See you soon.' I even find myself adding 'Love you!' which is weird, because until now I've always been too shy to say it. But it turns out she can't see me or hear me, because the nurse is still leaning over her bed. I leave the building wishing I'd said a proper goodbye.

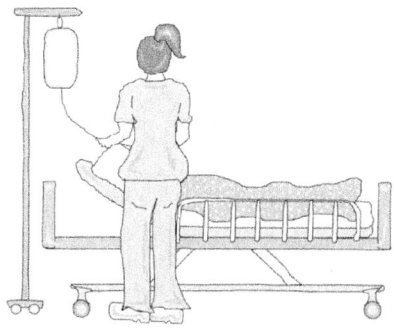

Milly calls me as soon as I'm home. 'Well? Did Granny Grub solve it?'

'Sort of. She reckons that the Grimbag and Snoop are hiding something. We need to search for it in the Grimbag's office.'

'Woah: that's a tough one. Where do we start?'

'How about another sleepover? We can figure out a plan without Trixie snooping around.'

'Sounds good. My house, tomorrow evening? It's my turn, anyway. And Dad's away as usual, so you don't have to face him just yet.'

'You're on!'

CHAPTER 62

Mobbs Manor

I'm heading to Milly's for the sleepover, wearing my newest jeans and top. But I still look like a walking jumble sale, especially compared to the fancy stuff Milly wears. Plus my hair's decided to go completely wild, so now the jumble sale clothes are topped by a massive frizz-ball.

Mum's given me a long list of *do*s and *don't*s:

DO say 'thank you for having me'.

DON'T slurp your drink.

DO offer to wash up.

DON'T leave your knickers lying around.

She's worried in case Mrs Mobbs thinks I'm badly brought up. The list goes on and on, so I'll spare you the rest.

I reach Milly's front gate, but it's not like the rusty little gate at the front of Granny's house; it's two massive gates that tower over me. I go to push them open, but they're jammed shut. How do I get in?

On each side, there's a stone lion, frozen in the middle of a roar. I reach out to feel their teeth, and they're sharp enough to scratch my fingers. A-ha: inside the mouth, there's a button, too. I press it, then quickly pull my hand away in case the jaws snap shut.

But nothing happens except a short buzzing noise. Have I got the wrong house?

I'm about to run away, when Milly's voice comes out of a speaker in the wall. 'Hi? Kayla?'

'No, it's Father Christmas. Blimey Mills, is this a house or a fortress? Let me in!'

The gates swing open and I walk through. But where's the house? All I see is a long drive, lined by trees. I set off along it, worried that I've gone the wrong way. Finally the drive turns a corner and the house appears. It's so big, it looks like lots of houses stuck together. Mrs Mobbs' red sports car is parked in front, shiny and gleaming.

'Hiya!' Milly runs out, smiling. She's wearing a trendy pair of jeans, with designer trainers to match.

'Mills, I always knew you were posh but you never told me you were rich.'

'Excuse me, but we're not that rich.'

'Because?'

'I have to chip in my own pocket money for riding lessons.'

I don't say anything.

An upstairs window opens and Billy leans out. 'Hi Kayla. Welcome to the World of Mobbs Misery! A special place, where mums don't care whether their kids live or die.' An ear-splitting noise blares out from behind him. It sounds like a truck crashing into a giant tin can, over and over again.

'Billy's latest protest,' sulks Milly. 'He says it's music, but there's nothing I can sing along to, no matter how hard I try.'

'I think it's called thrash metal,' I tell her, secretly impressed.

'If you say so,' she shrugs. 'Come on. Let's go up to my room.'

As she leads me upstairs, I can't help staring at everything. The hallway that's bigger than Granny's whole house. The staircase that looks like it's out of a film set. The long landing with so many doors, you can't tell which room's which.

Milly hammers angrily on one of the doors as we walk past, so I guess that's Billy's. In answer, the thrash metal dies down a bit, then Milly pulls me into her bedroom and shuts us inside.

Her room's so huge, you could hold Miss Hillock's hula-hoop lesson in here and still have room for the tug-of-war. There's even a second bed in the corner where I'm going to sleep. But something's missing. Or rather, someone.

'Hey Mills, where's Mr Bunnyfun?'

Milly bites her lip. 'Gone.'

'Gone where?'

'Mum got rid of him yesterday when I was at school.'

'No way! Why didn't you tell me?'

'I was too upset.'

'Which kids' charity did she give him to?'

'As if! She threw him out with the rubbish. He was murdered! Crushed to death, inside the rubbish van! And I didn't even have chance to say goodbye. I know I'm being a pathetic baby, but I'd swap my riding lessons for Mr Bunnyfun, any day.'

'I'm so sorry, Mills.'

'Really? You're not just saying that?'

'Mr Bunnyfun was a kind, helpful friend. I'm glad I got to meet him.'

That just makes her cry. She rests her head on my shoulder and now my top looks even worse because her nose has run all over it. But when you're besties, stuff like that doesn't matter.

She finally reaches the sniff-and-hiccup stage, and sits up straight again. 'I'll just have to grow up and get over it, like Mum says. Maybe one day, I'll learn to think of him as a silly old stuffed toy. But not yet, Kayla. I'm still too raw.' She gives herself a shake. 'No point crying over crushed bunnies. We need to come up with the next stage of our plan.'

We grab some pens and paper, and plonk down on her fluffy pink rug, ready to make a start.

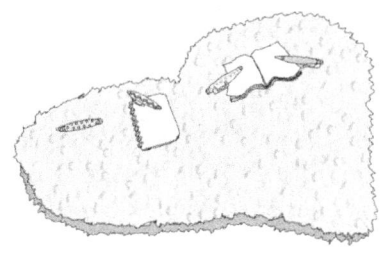

CHAPTER 63

Billy's Willing

Here's what I write down, and what Milly copies into her own notebook:

> *Task: Sneak into the Grimbag's office. Find out what she and Snoop are hiding.*
>
> *Problem: How do we sneak into a school we don't belong to?*
>
> *Solution: ???*

In the long silence that follows, I wrack my brains, while Milly happily doodles butterflies, rainbows and flowers. Then she leaps up with excitement. 'I've got it! We hire a helicopter and drop down on a rope, right into the Grimbag's office! I saw it in a movie and it's easy as anything. Plus we get to wear a black body-stocking! How cool is that?'

I don't want to hurt her feelings, especially so soon after Mr Bunnyfun's murder. 'Can we really afford a helicopter?' I begin gently. 'And what if we can't find body-stockings in our size?'

'Fine!' she sulks. 'In that case, why don't you just walk into the Grimbag's office all by yourself? Just toddle across the playground and in through the front door.'

'Only Swindel kids are allowed inside. You know that as well as I do. We need to approach this from a new angle.'

'Exactly!' she crows. 'And my angle is up above the office – hovering in the air!' She snatches up her phone and starts researching helicopter hire. Now I'm even more desperate to come up with a different plan, and a new idea bubbles up inside me. 'Hey Mills, what if I disguise myself as Billy? Wear his uniform?'

'That's just mad!'

'Madder than a helicopter? Look, we've only got two more days before Snoop comes back. If I'm gonna sneak into the Grimbag's office, I need to look like I belong to Swindel.'

'What if Billy won't lend you his clothes? He's in a tough place right now.'

As if to prove the point, there's a strange noise outside. A scrunch of gravel, a snapping of twigs, and a triumphant cry of 'Ha!'. Then it starts all over again: SCRUNCH-SNAP-HA! We rush to the window and spot Billy riding his bike through the flower beds, crushing the plants.

'Great,' sighs Milly. 'Another protest. At least this one won't kill him.'

'How long will it take him to trash the whole garden?'

'Oh, ages. There's loads more garden, round the back. Why d'you ask?'

'Cos if we're quick, I can try on his uniform without him knowing. See if it works.'

'I had a feeling you were gonna say that.' She leads me to his bedroom and closes the door behind us.

I'd forgotten that he'd painted his whole room black. Even though the daylight's still streaming through the window, everything looks murky. Milly mutters something about his appalling lack of taste, then flicks a light on.

We get down to business: I fling off my jeans, top and trainers, and scramble into Billy's uniform as fast as she throws it at me. Everything's a bit loose, because he's well-rounded and I'm skinny. But my Clods clothes are too big for me anyway, so I'm used to them slopping around. And the mirror shows me that I can get away with it.

Even Milly's impressed. 'Hello Billy!' she chuckles, tucking my hair into his cap. Flushed with success, I shove my hands into the blazer pockets, ready to practice striding up and down.

Hang on, what's this? Inside one of the pockets, there's a note in Billy's handwriting. On the front, it says *Protest and Survive*.

'D'you think we should read it?' asks Milly, nervously.

'Hmm. It's meant to be private.'

'Good point. There again…'

We both fly at the note and read it as quickly as our eyes will go:

Got to step up the danger, so Mum finally cracks!
Ideas:

1. Go to the aquarium and swim in the shark tank.

2. Become a stunt pilot. They often crash and kill themselves.

3. Become a bomb disposal expert. Good chance of blowing myself to pieces.

Need to choose – before Swindel kills me first.

Milly flinches, as if in pain. 'He's so desperate – and there's nothing we can do to help!'

'What the – ?!' exclaims Billy, standing in the doorway. He looks me up and down, then gawps at my clothes scattered everywhere, then stares at me all over again. I shove the note back in his pocket, but he sees me do it and looks ready to explode with anger.

'Awkward!' groans Milly, avoiding his eye.

'Is this how you both get your kicks?' he demands. 'You're sick, the pair of you!'

'We can explain!' insists Milly. 'Please, Bruv: just hear us out.'

He folds his arms and leans against the doorframe. 'Go on, then. It'd better be good.'

Milly nudges me forward, so I cross my fingers and launch in: 'It's not for kicks, Billy; it's a disguise. I need to sneak into the Grimbag's office.'

'Why?'

'Because we think she's hiding a Dirty Big Secret. If we can find out what it is, maybe we can stop her doing other bad things.'

'Like what?'

'Taking over Clods!' blurts out Milly, before slapping her hand over her mouth and throwing me a look that says 'Please don't kill me!'

'The Grimbag's getting her claws into Clods?' he gasps. 'Hasn't that woman wrecked enough lives, already?'

'You mustn't tell anyone,' Milly warns him.

'Yeah, like you just didn't,' he snorts. 'Hey, maybe the Dirty Big Secret will send her packing from Swindel too? Then I'll be a free man!' Now his eyes gleam with fresh hope. 'So you need to borrow my uniform? When d'you need it?'

'Tomorrow,' I reply keenly. 'When will her office be empty?'

'After school. That's when she'll be holding her Exams for Wimps class in the main hall. She keeps a firm grip on that class; she'll never leave it alone.'

'Cheers, Billy. Sounds like a plan!'

If only my mind wasn't already racing through a hundred things that could go wrong.

DONG! A bell sounds from downstairs – loud enough to make us jump. 'Tea's ready,' explains Billy. 'Mum always lets us know by whacking a bell with a hammer. She loves hitting things.'

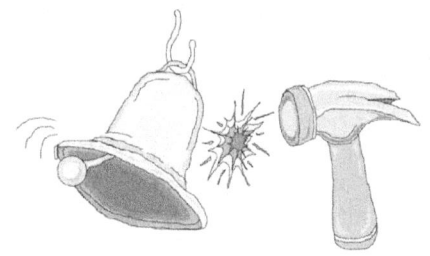

Milly bundles him onto the landing and shuts the door, so I can change back into my own clothes. I do it as quickly as I can, but he marches in again while I'm still straightening my top. 'Suits you,' he grins shyly. Milly rolls her eyes. 'Oh Kayla, will he ever learn to knock?' But she's grinning, too.

Mrs Mobbs crossly shouts from below: 'If you lot don't come down to tea this second, I'm throwing it away!' Milly pulls me aside. 'Listen, whatever happens next, I'm really sorry, ok?' It's not a good sign.

CHAPTER 64

Runaway Girl

Milly leads me to a dining room at the back of the house. It looks out on a huge garden, dotted with statues. There's a summer house too, plus a tennis court, a swimming pool, and a pond with a fountain.

If Billy hadn't trashed all the flower beds, it'd look perfect. But now the whole place is littered with broken plants and trails of mud, as if a bomb's gone off. 'Nice work!' murmurs Billy, pleased with himself.

Mrs Mobbs bursts in with a tray, determined to ignore the wrecked garden. She looks me up and down, from my cheap plastic hair-slide to the hole in my trainers. 'Well,' she sneers. 'You're not exactly dressed for dinner, but you might as well sit down. I suppose you're only here for the food, after all.'

'Mum!' gasp Milly and Billy together. 'Kayla's our friend!'

That gives me just enough courage to try and win her over. 'Good evening, Mrs Mobbs,' I begin sweetly. 'Thank you for letting me visit.' Mum would be dead pleased that I've said my first 'thank you' so quickly. It doesn't work, though: Mrs Mobbs just says 'Hmmff!' and stares at my hair, as if I made it frizzy on purpose.

On each placemat, there's a starched white cloth, twisted into a frilly shape. When Milly and Billy sit down, they shake it out and drape it over their knees.

Oh, so it's a napkin! I do my best to copy them, but what about when I've finished? Do I need to fold it back into that frilly shape? How the hell will I manage that?

'Salmon mousse on a bed of celery, drizzled with olive oil,' announces Mrs Mobbs, handing out the starter, which looks like something fancy you see on cookery shows.

We eat in gloomy silence. I try to chew my celery as quietly as possible, but it's deafening. Then my knife scrapes against the plate, and the sound echoes round the room. Finally they start chatting, but what they say is totally weird. It goes like this:

Mrs Mobbs: Millicent, will you ask William if he passed his exams today?

Milly: Bruv, Mum says did you pass your exams today?

Billy: Sis, will you tell Mum that I don't care if I pass 'em or not, cos I'd rather die than spend another week at Swindel?

Milly: Mum, Billy says he doesn't care if –

She doesn't get chance to finish, because Mrs Mobbs storms out of the room. Now I get it: Mrs Mobbs and Billy aren't speaking to each other, and poor Milly's the go-between.

Billy throws down his napkin and stomps upstairs. The thrash metal noise kicks in again, only this time he's strumming along on his banjo. Loud, angry chords that scream *Go to Hell!*

'I can't take much more of this,' wails Milly with a scared glance at the kitchen, where Mrs Mobbs is taking out her anger on some pots and pans. She soon bursts in with another tray and thrusts the plates at us, like weapons. 'Lemon-stuffed chicken,' she snarls,

'With honeyed baby carrots and a side dressing of smashed tomatoes.'

Even though the food's as posh as the house, Milly and I just pick at it. It's hard to feel hungry when the grim mood is sticking in our throats. I think back to Mum's list of do's and don't's. 'DO make polite conversation', she said. 'If in doubt, start with a compliment.'

I put down my knife and fork and put on my grown-up voice. 'What a wonderful home you have, Mrs Mobbs.' She looks at me sharply. 'Yes, I expect it does seem wonderful to someone like you.'

'Mum?' gulps Milly, shocked all over again.

'Spare me the attitude, Millicent. Kayla knows very well what I mean. A decent house and garden are bound to impress her lot.'

'MUM!' explodes Milly, now red with anger.

I can't pretend to be polite and grown-up anymore; I feel like something from the bottom of a toilet. If I don't escape this house right now, I'll be trapped in that feeling forever.

Without stopping to explain, I sprint upstairs, grab my bag, and rush out of the front door.

Milly runs after me, frantic. 'Kayla, I'm so sorry. She had no right to say that!'

'I did nothing wrong, Mills! Why does she hate the way I look and sound? I can't help being me!'

'Please don't go. Now that Mr Bunnyfun's dead, you're my only friend in the whole wide world!'

She reaches out to me, but I'm so hurt, I lash out at her. 'A proper friend would never invite me to such a madhouse!' I march off down the long drive, not looking back.

By the time I get home, it's nearly dark. 'Goodness, Kukoo!' begins Dad. 'Have you walked? All by yourself? At this hour? Anything could've happened! Please don't ever do that again!'

Mum takes off my coat. 'Have you and Milly fallen out? I hope that didn't stop you being nice and polite to Mrs Mobbs?' I mumble something about needing to do my homework, then disappear up to my room.

It feels lovely and safe to be back here, with Cleo curled up on my bed. I shove my homework out of sight, and snuggle down beside her for a chat.

She starts by opening one eye, as if to ask the obvious question: 'Why didn't you tell Mum and Dad the truth, just now? Don't they need to know about Mrs Mobbs? How she treated you?'

'I can't tell 'em, Cleo. What if they stormed over to her house and caused a scene? Then she'd say disgusting things to them, too. She'd give 'em the bottom-of-a-toilet feeling. They don't deserve that. I won't let it happen.'

She signals her approval by tapping me on the nose with her tail. 'Thanks, Cleo. You'll stick by me, won't you? Now that I've gone and blown it with Milly, you're the only friend I've got left.'

She opens her other eye, and the message comes across loud and clear. 'What about poor Milly? The toxic mum's not her fault. But you walked out, and now Milly's got no one. She can't even turn to Billy; he's too caught up in his own problems.'

That makes me think about things in a whole new way. Until this evening, I always wanted Milly's silky hair, skiing holidays, riding lessons and perfect school uniform. But I wouldn't swap with her, now. Because I've learnt some really sad things about her life: her mum doesn't love her; her brother's destroying himself; and her dad's never around.

'Y'know what, Cleo? I'm gonna try and make it up with Milly, first thing tomorrow. That OK with you?' She closes both eyes again, happy that she's made her point.

But will Milly forgive me? Will she and Billy still help me sneak into the Grimbag's office, after school? I need them now, more than ever.

CHAPTER 65

Truth Time

When Milly and I spot each other in the playground next morning, we both feel awkward.

'Kayla, there's something I need to say.'

'Me too.'

'You go first.'

'OK, Mills. The thing is: I'm sorry I walked out on you. You're as different from your mum as –'

'Toffee's different from lemons?'

'Yeah, spot on! She was dead lemony yesterday. So bitter, I had to spit her out and clear off.'

'Listen,' she frowns. 'I'm the one to blame. I knew that Mum would be like that. But I invited you anyway, cos I'm so lonely.'

We link arms, just like we used to, and stroll around the playground, closer than ever.

'Wish I had your parents,' she continues. 'The minute I met 'em, I wanted to swap with you.'

'Really? But they're so annoying! They make me wear this disgusting second-hand uniform. They fuss around me, like I'm a little kid. They don't even use my real name. What grown-up twelve year-old is ever called Kukoo?'

'Oh Kayla, that's nothing. They're the best mum and dad in the world. Because they really care about you.' Even Cleo didn't put it quite like that. It's a lot to think about.

Milly digs into her bag and hands me a posh box, tied with a ribbon. 'Here's your pudding from last night. I couldn't stop myself eating most of it, but what's left is yours.'

'Bless! What is it?'

'Well according to Mum, it's sponge fingers soaked in sherry, covered with fruit and custard, then topped with whipped cream.'

'Trifle, then?'

'Yeah. Trust Mum to make it sound poncy! And look: I've brought a spoon, in case you wanna share it?'

We tuck in, and don't notice Trixie until she snatches the spoon from Milly and waves it in the air. 'Guzzling again, Gut-Bucket? You really should cut down the calories, y'know. Or d'you wear a special elastic uniform that keeps expanding?'

Milly tries to grab the spoon back, but Trixie smirks and waves it higher. Now Milly's wild with rage and yells in Trixie's face: 'Give it here, Trixie Minx! Or should I say Trixie *Grimm*?'

Trixie looks like she's been struck by lightning. 'Trixie wh-who?' she stammers, dropping the spoon to the ground.

'Oh, you heard me well enough,' retorts Milly. 'We know the real you – so there!'

Trixie shoots us a look of pure hatred. 'Sneaky, stinking spies – the pair of you!'

'Just a little detective work,' crows Milly. 'Maybe we're not losers, after all.'

'Ooh, aren't you nice 'n' smug?' snarls Trixie. 'But you can drop it right now. Cos if you ever tell anyone about me, your lives won't be worth living. You've no idea how deadly I can be. Don't make me prove it.' She snatches the trifle and hurls it at our feet, then slips away without another word.

Now Milly looks ready to cry, and it's not about the trifle. 'I've blabbed!' she wails. 'Yet again! Why can't I keep my stupid mouth shut?'

'She really got to you, Mills. You couldn't help hitting back.'

'True,' she sniffs. 'There are only so many Gut-Bucket jokes a girl can take.'

While she blows her nose, I scoop up the trifle and throw it in the bin. 'How bad is it?' asks Milly.

'Covered in grit.'

'No, I mean how bad is the situation? Trixie knows that our spying is getting us somewhere.'

'Yeah, but she doesn't know about sneaking into the Grimbag's office. You managed not to blab that bit.'

Milly takes my arm again. 'Good point. Billy's gonna meet us straight after school, so you can change into his uniform. And remember we've still got the back-up plan.'

'Errr...?'

'Helicopter hire! It's just one call away.'

If only I felt so confident. As the day drags on, I'm so nervous I have to keep running to the toilet.

What if I'm caught before I reach the Grimbag's office? And what if her Dirty Big Secret's not there, anyway? How will I stop her and Snoop from ruining my family's life?

R–ing! Ri–! R–! It's the end of school. Time to go and meet Billy, and get the plan underway.

CHAPTER 66

Suits You

Milly grabs her phone. 'Clothes swap, here we come. Where shall I tell Billy to meet us?'

'How about the Clods dustbins?'

'But they stink!'

'Exactly. We'll have 'em all to ourselves.'

She messages Billy and he replies with two emojis: a stinking poo, and a laugh-till-you-cry.

Milly's harder to win over: by the time we reach the bins, she's shuddering with disgust. 'Gross!' she grumbles. 'They're not just stinky; they're farty. Especially that one at the end.'

'The fartier, the better.'

'Kayla, are you a brilliant detective, or just plain weird? I still can't work it out.'

'Where's Billy? Shouldn't he be here by now?'

'Don't worry; leave that bit to me.'

I thought she'd message him, but instead she calls out: 'Has Miss Jellybean landed on the moon?'

'What's going on, Mills? Who's Miss Jellybean? And what's the moon got to do with anything?'

'Shhh!' she hisses. 'It's a password. Billy and I agreed it, earlier. I ask the Jellybean question and he gives the secret answer. That way, we know it's each other.'

'Can't you just call out his name? Or peep behind the bins and see if he's there?'

'Look, in the books and films they always have a special password, OK? D'you wanna do this thing properly or not?'

'Sorry. You go ahead.'

She tries again: 'Has Miss Jellybean landed on the moon?'

This time, a grisly croak emerges from the farty bin at the end: 'Yes, thanks to her jelly-powered rocket.'

She stamps her foot. 'Stop it, Bruv! Why are you putting on that stupid voice?' His face pops round the side. 'It's a scary vibe, to get us all in the mood. Come and join me, ladies. Farty but cosy!'

'You or the bin?' she chuckles, as we creep around the back.

He's sitting on an upturned bucket with his banjo case across his knees, and he's still wearing his Swindel uniform. 'Hello?' Milly snaps at him. 'We need your uniform right now. Why haven't you changed into your spare clothes?'

'Can't,' he squirms. 'Forgot to bring 'em.'

'Typical! Well in that case, just change into Kayla's uniform, once she's taken it off.'

'You think I'm gonna wear a skirt? No way! Not for anything or anyone.'

'Fine. Just hang about in your underpants.'

'As if!'

They glare at each other, trying not to blink.

I try a different tack. 'Billy, you hate the skirt idea. I get that. But don't you hate the Grimbag even more? She's wrecking your life, remember? Back-to-back exams. No lunch. And having to play the banjo faster and faster, until your fingers fall off!'

He's already loosening his tie. 'Y'know what? That skirt's gonna suit me just fine. On with the skirt; out with the Grimbag!'

We hide behind opposite bins to undress, and Milly passes the clothes between us. In no time at all, the swap is complete: I'm now a Swindel boy, and Billy's a Clods girl. 'Looking good!' grins Milly.

Oh, but I'd forgotten that my uniform has some nasty secrets of its own. Billy was bound to find out, and no wonder he's looking puzzled. 'Why are the sleeves so long?' he begins, unrolling them until they dangle down to his knees.

'No time for that now,' Milly tells him, giving me an apologetic smile.

'OK, but why's the skirt held up with a safety pin?'

'Enough already!' Milly warns him.

'OK, but why are the shoes stuffed with newspaper?'

Milly looks at me, shocked. 'You've got newspaper in your shoes?'

'Yeah. To keep 'em from falling off.'

'Why didn't you tell me?'

'You never noticed. And why would I show you?'

A pained look shoots across her face. 'Listen, why don't I buy you a new uniform? It's really no trouble.'

She means well, but I flush with shame. 'It doesn't feel right. And Mum and Dad wouldn't let you.'

'But –'

'Kayla always looks brilliant!' interrupts Billy. 'Better than anyone. End of story.'

Now I blush even redder, but this time it's with pride. Billy's praise is worth having. And I can tell he's not making it up; he looks so earnest, even though he's standing there in my skirt. 'Thanks,' I whisper.

They both help me to finish my 'Billy' look: buttoning my blazer and tying my laces with Swindel neatness. Then I scrunch my frizz-ball hair into Billy's cap and jam it down onto my head.

'Ready for battle!' declares Milly. 'And don't worry, Kayla: all that purple is bound to hide any bloodstains.'

Bloodstains? Oh my god! What am I getting into? I try to speak with a swagger. 'If I'm not back in an hour, just go home and pretend this never happened.'

'Tricky,' chuckles Billy. 'I'll still be wearing your clothes. Not sure how I'll explain that to Mum.'

Great. Now I don't just feel scared; I feel stupid, too. I head out of the Clods gates, turn into the Swindel playground, and carry on walking until I'm through the front door.

CHAPTER 67

Dragon's Den

The corridor's empty, but a shrill woman's voice rings out from a room at the end: 'I won't tolerate any wimps at Swindel; only winners! Especially when it comes to exams. So stop being a bunch of pathetic wimps, and learn to win, win, win!'

That can only be the Grimbag, leading her Exams for Wimps class. Perfect! Her office will be empty, like Billy promised.

I've barely taken another step, when a couple of teachers emerge from a classroom and head straight towards me. I turn my face to the wall and pretend to study one of the posters. *Join the Swindel Sports Squad!* it says. *We push you so hard, you throw up!*

One of the teachers slaps me on the back as they pass. 'Good for you, Boy! I'll expect to see you there tomorrow. With luck, we'll have you throwing up before you've even got your trainers on.'

'Can't wait!' I reply. 'I'll be sure to bring a sick-bag.'

They stroll off, murmuring something about my promising Swindel spirit. This school is even more toxic than I thought. The sooner I get to the Grimbag's office, the better.

I head up the stairs, just like Billy told me. They lead straight to a door with a warning sign:

*Headquarters of Supreme Commander
Grimm. Enter at Your Own Risk!*

Well at least I've found the right place. I spring inside and close the door behind me.

It's the tidiest room I've ever seen – because it's almost empty. There's just a long glass desk, a sleek computer and a massive leather chair. How the hell can I look for clues, when there's nothing here? Granny said that this office would be full of secrets, but it's full of nothing at all.

I feel like I've been kicked in the guts. What a waste of time! My whole plan is dead, and there's no time to try anything else. I take one last look around me, just for the memory. Will I ever have an office like this? Not now the Grimbag's won. Me and my family are finished.

Hey, but she can't stop me trying out that big leather chair. I go over and sit in it, just to spite her. It makes me feel like the boss, so I put my feet on the desk, and swivel round to address my imaginary team of assistants.

That's when the chair decides to take over: it jerks backwards, pointing me at the ceiling. If Milly saw me now, she'd die laughing. I kick my legs and clutch at the desk, to flip the chair back into position.

I must have clutched at the mouse too, because the computer screen flicks into life. Ooh, and it's showing a list of the Grimbag's emails:

Ruling the World in Three Easy Steps.
Nasty Things to Say to Pupils, Part 2.
Do Stiff Collars Make Me Look Powerful?
Nasty Things to Say to Teachers, Part 5.

Maybe the Dirty Big Secret's in here, somewhere? I quickly scroll through the list, but nothing jumps out at me. What shall I do? I haven't got time to read them all.

I try one more scroll, right to the bottom. The very last title makes my pulse race like a sprinter on steroids: *Clods Takeover: Nearly There!*

I click it open and can hardly believe what it says:

> ***Snoop****: Prepare to celebrate, this Friday! That's when I'll give the final FAIL to Clods, and we'll announce your takeover.*
>
> ***Grimm****: Excellent! PS. Did you remember to fix this year's exam results? Swindel must always come out on top, you know.*
>
> ***Snoop****: Yes, I've boosted your scores, as always. A simple matter of hacking into the central computer.*
>
> ***Grimm****: Nice work. Did you also remember to downgrade the Clods results? It's extra-special when they're bottom of the table.*
>
> ***Snoop****: Yes, all sorted. But none of this will top your own masterstroke, from years ago.*
>
> ***Grimm****: Ah yes, swapping the Clods teachers into the wrong jobs. Oh, how Pippa hated it! But of course she had no choice. And she's been stuck with it, ever since.*
>
> ***Snoop****: Anything else you need from me?*
>
> ***Grimm****: Yes: Trixie must get top marks.*

Snoop: *Even though she's at Clods? Well don't worry; she's the only Clods pupil who'll pass. I'll give her straight A's.*

Grimm: *You're worth every penny, Snoopy.*

Snoop: *Glad you agree, Gabbykins. Did you transfer the money into my account?*

Grimm: *I know your price, and I've paid it.*

Snoop: *And you'll make me your Deputy Head? Don't forget that's part of the deal.*

Grimm: *Of course. Between us, we'll turn Swindel and Clods into our personal powerbase. Riches and fame will follow – you just wait!*

It's the Dirty Big Secret. Yes, the Clods teachers are in each other's jobs – and now I know why: it's because THE GRIMBAG MADE THEM SWAP!

Granny was right: she knew I'd find the clues here. The Grimbag and Snoop are dangerous crooks, hooked on a crazy power trip.

But no one will believe me unless I can prove it. Why didn't I think to borrow Milly's phone? I could have taken a shot of the Grimbag's screen. I'll just have to print out the email. Easy! Or so I think.

CHAPTER 68

Print & Run

For the first few seconds, it goes well: I press Print and a machine under the desk starts humming. Then – CLANK! – it grinds to a halt. I crouch down to read the screen: *PRINTER JAM. Clear paper and try again.*

I'm running out of time: the Grimbag will be back any minute. I fumble with the printer, pulling out the mangled scraps of paper and stuffing them into my pocket. I close the lid and press Print once more. Now the screen says *OUT OF PAPER. Refill and try again.*

Damn! Where in this empty office can I find spare paper? I spot a drawer under the desk and open it. Yes! There's a whole stack of paper, arranged in a perfectly neat block. I snatch a couple of sheets and feed them into the printer. It whirrs into life but then stops and says *OUT OF TONER. Replace ink cartridge and try again.*

No, no, NO!!! This printer's pure evil. There's no time to look for the ink, but I *have* to print that email. I give the printer a good, hard thump – to teach it a lesson. The top flies off and it starts printing. The words are almost too faint to read, but it'll have to do.

By the time the full page appears, I've already wrestled the top of the printer back into place. I snatch up the page and rush to the door, ready to escape. But a couple of voices stop me dead. They're in the corridor, just outside.

'Trixie my girl! Shouldn't you be hanging around at Clods? You're meant to be spying on your Auntie Pippa.'

'I've come to tell you something.'

'Go on.'

'This morning, the fattest girl in my class called me Trixie Grimm!'

'What?! How did she find out?'

'I reckon her bestie told her.'

'I suppose you mean her best friend. How did *she* find out?'

'This other girl's clever. Her parents work at Clods and she wants Auntie Pippa to stay on as Head. She's the one who found out about Snoopy's first visit, and wrote those notes I told you about.'

'That list of tips for the teachers?'

'Yeah. And now she knows my secret, too.'

'But how did she find out about Snoop's visit?'

'Maybe she found a clue in Auntie Pippa's office. She's been sneaking around in there, when she thinks I'm not looking.'

'Well at least she can't snoop around here!'

'Yeah. She'll never know about the exam fixing, or your takeover plans.'

'Oh Trixie, why didn't you get rid of her at the start?'

'D'you think I didn't try? I like to think I'm a pretty good bully, but she's stuck around.'

'In that case, your bullying wasn't up to scratch.'

'Should I go back and bully harder? Bully meaner?'

'Actually, no. Until Snoopy comes back this Friday, you need to stop bullying this girl. Be friends instead.'

'Friends? Yuck!'

'Yes, not pleasant. But this girl sounds dangerous, and we don't want her telling anyone else about our connection. At least not until I've taken over Clods. Then I'll boot her out, myself.'

'Ha ha! Nice one, Mum!'

'Now get along home. But no need to bother with homework; Snoopy's fixed your A-grades.'

'Cheers, Mum. Will you walk me across the playground?'

'You're not a baby, Trixie.'

'But I'm wearing this stupid Clods uniform. What if I'm bullied by your lot?'

I creep to the window and watch them walk to the front gate. Time to escape. I sprint out of the office, down the stairs and along the corridor. Nearly there!

'Where d'you think you're going, young man? Running away from my Exams for Wimps class?'

It's the Grimbag! She's back in the front entrance, blocking my way!

We begin a deadly game of dodge: I go to squeeze past and she reaches out to grab me. She misses me by a whisker, but snatches my cap and my hair tumbles out. Her shrill voice carries across the playground as I sprint away. 'Hey, who are you? Swindel boys have decent, respectable haircuts! Come back here, this minute!'

I keep running until I'm back at Clods, out of sight.

CHAPTER 69
Magic Words

Approaching the Clods dustbins, I hear the sound of a banjo. Compared to the Grimbag's shrieks, it's music to my ears.

Milly's hidden behind the bins, but hears my footsteps and calls out: 'Halt! Password please.'

I heave a weary sigh. 'Look, I've been through a lot since you last saw me. Can we skip the password nonsense?'

'No. Sorry.'

'In that case, you'll have to give me a hint.'

'OK, it's something to do with sweets and space.'

'I've got it! Has Miss Marshmellow landed in her spaceship?'

'Sorry Kayla; not even close.'

'Ha! You just said *Kayla*, so you know it's me. Can we drop the password now?'

'Nice try, but no.'

I have another go. 'Has Miss Bubblegum landed in her flying saucer?'

'Still wrong, but I'll accept it or we'll be here all night.'

That annoys me so much, I decide to take revenge. 'Haven't you forgotten something, Mills? You need to give me the secret answer.'

'Ha! You just said *Mills*, so you know it's me!'

'But I still had to give you the password, even though you'd already said *Kayla*.'

'Oh, if you insist. Yes, thanks to her jelly-powered rocket. Satisfied?'

'But we've switched to Miss Bubblegum, so jelly doesn't fit anymore.'

Milly pops her head out. 'D'you have to be so picky? Billy and I are dying to know what happened. Come and tell us, before we kill you.'

I join them round the back of the bins, and Billy plays an upbeat tune to welcome me back. I can tell he's not used to wearing a skirt, because he's sitting with his legs apart and the banjo doesn't quite hide his underpants. It's hard not to look.

Milly's exploding with impatience. 'So? Any Dirty Big Secrets?' I hand her the print-out and she scans it, wide-eyed. But all she says is: 'They call each other Gabbykins and Snoopy? That's my worst nightmare. And believe me, I dream some pretty weird stuff.'

Billy seems absorbed in his playing, so I pull her to one side. 'Mills, those emails are a dead giveaway! It was the Grimbag who swapped our teachers into each other's jobs! And why? To make Clods look rubbish. With Snoop's help, she even fixes the exam results, to put Swindel top and Clods bottom. Oh, but Trixie's different: the Grimbag's giving her straight A's. She's paying Snoop secret money, and she's gonna make him Deputy Head!'

Billy calls out: 'Thanks for the update, Kayla!'

I let out a long, slow groan. Me and my big mouth.

Milly grips my hand. 'My fault. I should've warned you. He can play and listen at the same time.'

'My only true skill,' adds Billy, striking a fresh tune to prove his point.

'You mustn't ever tell anyone,' Milly warns him. 'If you do, I'll take a pair of scissors and cut off your banjo strings. I mean it!'

'Ouch! You sure know how to hurt a guy. But no worries. From what Kayla says, it sounds like you've got the Grimbag cornered. Why would I go and spoil it?'

Milly nods her approval, but still pulls me aside for the next bit. 'Any sign of Trixie?'

'Yeah. She told the Grimbag that we know about the mother-daughter thing.'

'What did the Grimbag say?'

'She told Trixie to be nice to us. But only until Snoop visits this Friday. Then she'll boot me out.'

Milly bristles with anger. 'Well *they're* the ones who are gonna get booted out, and all thanks to these emails. They're dynamite!'

I nod back at her, pleased with myself for once. Billy stops playing. 'Hey Kayla, where's my cap?' Now my self-belief plummets like a stone falling off a cliff. 'Sorry, Billy. The Grimbag's got it. She snatched it as I ran out the door.'

'Hmm,' he frowns. 'Did she see your face?'

'Don't think so, but she shouted something about haircuts.'

'We'll just have to make sure she never spots you again. Your amazing hair will always give you away.'

Even though I'm still mad with myself, a little spark lights up inside me. He called my hair 'amazing'!

'And no worries about the cap,' he smiles. 'I'll think of an excuse to tell Mum. In fact I'll enjoy lying to her.'

'Won't she shout and scream?'

'Yeah, like crazy. But then she'll go straight out and buy me a new one. Anything to keep me at Swindel.'

We go to our opposite dustbins to get changed, and Milly goes back to handing the clothes between us. 'What happens now?' she asks me. 'Are you gonna show the emails to Miss Skipper?'

'Yeah. First thing tomorrow.'

'How will you explain how you got 'em?'

'Dunno. Maybe Cleo will help me come up with something?'

'Fine, so long as you don't tell Miss Skipper that you've done another break-in. You're in enough trouble, already.'

'Thanks for the skirt,' grins Billy. 'I enjoyed it, in the end.'

Milly gives him a playful shove. 'Glad you discovered a new side of yourself!'

I can't wait to tell Granny that her idea was a total brainwave. But I won't visit her this evening. I'll wait until I've seen Miss Skipper. Then I'll tell Granny everything.

CHAPTER 70

Know All

R–ing! Ri–! R–! It's Thursday: just one more day until Snoop comes back. I head to Miss Skipper's office, first thing.

She's sitting at her desk, reading her library book (*How to Deal With a Crisis and Still Be a Nice Person*) and scribbling away on post-it notes. The notes are stuck all over the desk and walls, so she must be finding the book very helpful.

She looks up, annoyed at being disturbed. 'Yes, Kayla? What is it this time?' I don't say anything; I just hand over the email. The page got torn and crumpled during my escape, and the ink seems fainter than ever, but you can still read it if you screw up your eyes.

She reads it in silence, her eyes screwed so tight they're almost shut. 'How did you get hold of this?' she asks, quietly.

I trot out the lines that I rehearsed this morning, in front of the mirror. 'You'll never believe me, Miss, but that piece of paper blew out of Mrs Grimm's office window, flew across the playground, and landed on me when I was walking past their front gate.'

'You're right, Kayla: I don't believe you. Do you take me for an idiot? Let me tell you what actually happened. You're friends with Milly Mobbs, whose brother Billy goes to Swindel. Billy visited Mrs

Grimm's office for some reason, and spotted this piece of paper. He then handed it over to you, so you could pass it on to me. Correct?'

'Yes Miss,' I lie. It's not the full truth, of course, but it's much better than my stupid 'flew out of the window' story.

'Apart from you and Milly and Billy, does anyone else know what Mrs Grimm is up to?'

'Sort of, Miss,' I squirm.

'For goodness' sake, Kayla: yes or no? And if it's a yes, then who?'

'Trixie, Miss. She's on Mrs Grimm's side. The side that's trying to destroy Clods.'

She flops back in her chair, all washed out. 'Kayla, I already knew that Trixie passed your teachers' notes to Inspector Snoop. But I decided to regard this as a one-off mistake. Surely she can't be against us, too?'

"Fraid so, Miss. Billy overheard her talking to Mrs Grimm about it.' It wasn't Billy, as you know: it was me – but once you start lying, you can't stop.

She looks at me sharply. 'What else did Billy hear?'

'When Trixie spoke to Mrs Grimm, she didn't call her *Mrs Grimm* at all. She used a very different name.'

'And that name was…?'

'Mum.'

It's as though I've shot her with a stun-gun. Is she even breathing? After a long pause she blinks and swallows and looks at me again. 'Congratulations, Kayla: you've got closer than anyone else to finding out the truth. And that makes me wonder something rather surprising.'

'D'you mean, why am I such an idiot at other stuff? Like algebra and French verbs?'

'No,' she smiles. 'I'm wondering whether to tell you the full story. In any case, it's bound to get out soon. And in the meantime, you might help me to see the problem in a new way. You are a one-off, you know.'

'Thanks, Miss. I do my best.'

'Very well. Shall we make ourselves comfortable?' She shows me to the squishy old sofa in the corner of her office, and sits down beside me.

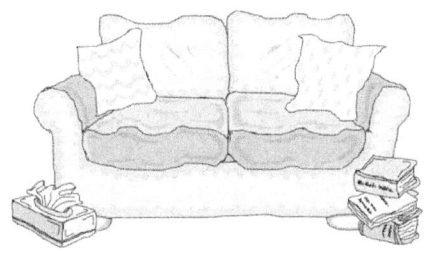

CHAPTER 71

Sister Story

Miss Skipper takes a deep breath and begins. 'The first thing you need to know is that Gabby Grimm and I are sisters. Trixie is Gabby's daughter, and my niece.'

My look of surprise obviously works, because she continues her story. 'Gabby and I came to school here at Clods. I was awarded numerous certificates and trophies, and my proud parents displayed them all over the house. But my sister Gabby never received any, and I'm afraid this made her jealous. Ever since then, she's tried to destroy me.'

'Why, Miss?'

'Because she wants to show that she can do better than me. I've often tried to talk to her about it, but she shuts me out. It's the biggest unhappiness of my life.'

She goes over to the window and gazes out. 'When I decided to become a teacher, Gabby chose that job too, determined to teach at a more impressive school. When I became Head of Clods, I knew that sooner or later, she'd take over Swindel.'

'When did she jumble up the Clods teachers, Miss?'

'Some years ago, I had to spend a week away on a training course. I even remember the title: *Are You Too Nice For Your Own Good?* Head Office put Gabby in charge of Clods that week. And that's when she had a horribly clever idea: find out each teacher's worst subject, and make them teach it.'

'Why didn't they tell her where to stick her stupid idea?'

'Oh they tried, of course. But she found ways to bully each and every one of them. Her techniques are savage, Kayla. In the end, they didn't dare protest.'

'But couldn't *you* stop it, Miss? Report her to Head Office?'

She catches her reflection in the wonky mirror and gazes at herself steadily, as though she's baring her soul. 'I knew that if I spoke up, it would land Gabby in deep trouble – and might lead her to cause even more damage. I couldn't live with that. So I chose to protect her and keep quiet.'

'But Miss, why didn't you just swap the teachers back again? Easy enough, after just one week!'

'Ah, but Gabby bullied me, too. She told me that if I swapped the teachers back, she'd never speak to our parents again. You look surprised, Kayla.'

'I don't mean to be rude, Miss. But I can't believe that you and Mrs Grimm still have parents!'

'Because we're so very old, you mean?' she asks, rejoining me on the sofa. 'My mother and father are indeed elderly, but still very much alive. I couldn't bear to think of them not seeing their younger daughter anymore. It'd break their hearts.'

'So Mrs Grimm's blackmailing you, Miss?'

'Yes, Kayla, it's blackmail: threatening to do something vicious, unless your demands are met.' She stands up again and paces about the room. 'So now you have the full story. I let my sister get away with it, even though it meant failing my pupils, my teachers and my whole school. You can judge me as harshly as you like. I know I deserve it.'

I have a quiet think. Miss Skipper's not a bad person. In fact she's one of the nicest people I've ever met. She just had an impossible choice. Finally I speak up. 'Y'know what, Miss? I'd have done the same if I was you.'

She sniffs back a tear. '*If **I were** you*, not *if **I was** you*. But thank you, Kayla. That means a lot.' She looks again at the emails and simmers with quiet anger. 'I'd no idea she was fixing the exam results, or paying Inspector Snoop to close us down. Nor did I realise that she sent Trixie here to cause trouble. This time, Gabby's gone too far.'

'And you can still stop her, Miss! She says she'll never speak to your parents again, but if she tries to cut 'em off, I reckon they'll still find a way to get through to her.'

'You really think so, Kayla?'

'Well *my* parents are pretty annoying, but I've gotta admit they always get through to me in the end. Like moving to this town, to look after Granny. At first, I hated the idea, even though I love Granny as much as anyone. But now I realise they were right, all along.'

She dabs her eyes with a hankie then clasps her hands together, squashing the hankie between them. 'Kayla Grub, I knew you'd shine a new light on this problem! Yes, it's time to put Clods first for a change. I've underestimated my parents. They *will* talk Gabby round! She'll always be part of their lives!'

'But Miss, how can you fix everything in time? Snoop's coming back tomorrow!'

She seizes a new stack of post-its and starts scribbling away. 'Can you and Milly come to my staff meeting this afternoon, straight after school? There's something I'd like you both to witness.'

'Your big fix plan?' I ask hopefully.

'Wait and see.' She thinks I've already gone, because when she looks up again a few minutes later, she jumps with surprise. 'For goodness' sake, Kayla: haven't you got lessons to go to?'

'There's something else that needs fixing, Miss.'

'If it's that blocked toilet on the second floor, then don't worry: your father's already booked a plumber for later today.'

'It's not the toilet, Miss. Although to be fair, it is a bit of a nightmare. The smell comes through the air vent, into Mrs Parler's classroom. Her last cookery class had to be abandoned, cos her Sherry Shrimps smelt like –'

'Kayla!' she interrupts crossly. 'Can you please get to the point?'

'Sorry, Miss. What I mean is, can you please fix Swindel while you're at it? It's tearing Billy to pieces. The other kids hate it too.'

'Didn't I already say wait and see? Now would you mind leaving me in peace? I have much to sort out. And please leave Trixie to me; I'll deal with her in my own way.' She goes back to scribbling on her post-its, so I creep away and leave her to it.

CHAPTER 72

Swap Back

R–ing! Ri–! R–! As soon as our final lesson's over, Milly and I head to the staffroom. I've told her all about my chat with Miss Skipper, and she can hardly believe it. 'So Miss Skipper's working on a big fix?' she asks me, excitedly.

'Hope so.'

'Don't suppose it involves helicopters?'

'Doubt it.'

'Body-stockings?'

'Unlikely.'

'Shame.'

We pause at the staffroom door, nervous to go in. Last time we were here, we set off the fire alarm, stuffed our notes into the teachers' bags, hid in the cupboard and escaped through the window. We creep inside, wondering how we ever escaped jail.

Miss Skipper must have warned the teachers that we're coming, because they don't throw us out. Even so, they give us some pretty hard stares, as if to say 'what the hell is this meeting about?'

Miss Skipper arrives at last, looking brisk and confident. 'Good afternoon, everyone. I'm sure you're wondering why I've asked two of our pupils to join us today. Let me explain. I've decided to launch the Clods Club. It's open to anyone who wants to help make our wonderful school even better. You'll be hearing a lot more about this in due course. But for now, allow me to introduce its first two members: Kayla Grub and Milly Mobbs.'

We actually get a round of applause! Milly steps forward and I realise with horror that she's about to curtsey and blow kisses to everyone. I pull her back, only just in time. 'Spoil sport!' she grumbles.

'Now to the main matter of the meeting,' continues Miss Skipper. 'Forgive me, but I'm going to put this bluntly: YOU'RE ALL IN THE WRONG JOBS!'

The teachers look dismayed but not surprised, as if they've expected this for a long time. 'So we're fired?' several of them ask, gloomily.

'Certainly not!' she exclaims. 'Because it's not your fault; it's mine. When Mrs Grimm swapped you round all those years ago, I should have undone her meddling as soon as I returned. But I failed to do so, for personal reasons that I'm afraid I can't disclose.'

She glances in my direction and I give her a smile that says 'You're doing great!' I'm not sure if she even sees me, but when she turns back to the teachers, her voice fills the whole room. 'I can't tell you how sorry I am for putting you all in that situation. You've all battled on bravely, but it's now time to put things right.' She pulls out a flipchart from her bag and pins it to the wall:

The Big Job Swap. Starting Tomorrow.

1. Mr Kulla: science → art
   Miss Zinc: art → science

2. Mr Prior: computer tech → history
   Mrs Hacker: history → computer tech

    3. Mr Figger: drama → maths
       Mr Props: maths → drama

    4. Mrs Choon: English language → music
       Miss Wurdy: music → English language

    5. Mr Champion: geography → games
       Miss Hillock: games → geography

    6. Mr Platter: French → cookery
       Mrs Parler: cookery → French

There's a stunned silence. Milly whispers 'Easy, now it's written down! Who knew?' I just hope I'm the only one who hears.

Finally, Mr Platter clears his throat and speaks up. 'Miss Skipper, I've always known that I'm the world's worst French teacher. But I never said anything, because I thought that all the other teachers were doing brilliantly.'

'Extraordinary!' exclaims Mrs Hacker. 'I thought that I was the only one who couldn't teach my new subject. I only kept quiet because I assumed that everyone else was doing well.'

'Bizarre!' declares Miss Wurdy. 'I thought that I was the only disaster and that everyone else was bound to be amazing. So I never spoke up.'

'It's true,' sighs Miss Skipper. 'Each of you imagined yourself to be the only failure. You were too ashamed to let me know. And having lost your confidence, you didn't dare seek a job elsewhere. So this wretched situation dragged on.'

The teachers all nod, startled into a new understanding.

'I've known all of this from the start,' continues Miss Skipper. 'Which is why I'm the one to blame. If you all wish to resign, I simply ask that you let me know, here and now. I'll be heartbroken to see you go, but I will understand.'

The teachers swap glances, but the room remains so silent, we can hear the clock ticking in the corridor.

'Goodness!' gasps Miss Skipper, now dangerously close to tears. 'Then dare I hope that... you all intend... to stay?'

Mr Props steps forward with a big gesture, as if he's on stage. 'Miss Skipper, I hope I speak for everyone here, when I say that I intend to stay for a long time yet. All I ever wanted was to get back to my old job!'

There's a chorus of 'Absolutely!' 'Me too!' 'Can't wait!'

Miss Skipper's tears fall openly now, but she whisks them away with her hankie and clasps it to her chest. 'I thank you with all my heart. You've given Clods a bright new future! Shall we celebrate with a cup of tea?'

CHAPTER 73

Tea Party

The staff meeting turns into a little party. In-between gulping down gallons of tea, the teachers chat away to each other, looking happier and more relaxed than I've ever seen them before.

When Miss Skipper spots Milly and me shyly lurking in the corner, she approaches us with an encouraging smile and two tins of biscuits. 'Will you please hand these round? And do help yourselves.'

Milly decides to stay in the corner with her tin. 'Miss Skipper did say help yourself!' she tells me, her mouth stuffed full of Ginger Nuts. But the teachers are staring at us, so I reckon one of us needs to get out there.

I shuffle into the crowd and manage to call out 'Custard Creme?' They empty my tin in no time, and I get to hear what they're saying.

Mr Platter and Mrs Parler are busy teaching each other the subjects they're actually good at. He's telling her why boiling water doesn't magically turn into jam; and she's telling him why you shouldn't speak French as though it's choking you. 'If only we'd known these things before,' they agree. 'We wouldn't have made such a mess of each other's jobs!'

Mr Kulla is handing his scientist's white coat to Miss Zinc. 'I never deserved to wear this,' he tells her. 'You're its true and rightful owner.' 'And I never deserved to wear these,' she replies, removing the paintbrushes from her hair and handing them over to him. 'They belong in the hands of a true artist!'

Miss Hillock and Mr Champion are competing for 'most awkward moment in each other's job'. 'I thought that tennis had to be played with ping-pong bats,' she groans. 'No wonder we kept losing to Swindel!' 'Mine's worse!' he squirms. 'I told my geography class that we're sitting on a volcano. No wonder they all looked so worried!'

When Milly's eaten every last biscuit and everyone's ready to leave, Miss Skipper makes a final announcement. 'Attention, please! Tomorrow we have a special visitor.'

The teachers cry out in alarm. 'Oh Miss Skipper! Not that dreadful Inspector Snoop?'

'I'm afraid so,' she replies. 'But this time it's different: you're all back in the right jobs! And who knows: you might even enjoy showing him what you can do?' It's a good point. They stop protesting and start swapping plans.

Then Mr Props steps forward once again, and speaks with the rich, booming voice of a professional actor. 'Forgive me, Miss Skipper, but I have to ask. Did you write me a note to try and help me pass his last inspection?'

The other teachers all cry out in surprise. 'You got a note too? I thought it was just me!'

'Yes, you all received a note,' replies Miss Skipper. 'And yes, they all carried my name. But I was not the author.'

'Then who was?' asks Miss Wurdy.

'A couple of well-wishers who wish to remain anonymous,' answers Miss Skipper, coolly. Milly and I go so red, the teachers all turn to look at us. Which makes us go even redder.

Miss Skipper helpfully creates a distraction by clanking two teacups together. 'Let's focus on the future, shall we? I expect you'd all like to get home and prepare for a successful day tomorrow.'

I'm keen to get home for a different reason: I can finally tell the whole story to Granny. I phone her as soon as I'm through the door. 'Hey Granny, guess what? I found the Dirty Big Secret in Mrs Grimm's office, just like you said! I've told Miss Skipper all about it, and she's busy fixing the Clods problem. She hasn't mentioned Swindel yet, but I reckon she's got something up her sleeve.'

Her voice sounds so faint I can hardly hear her reply, but it's something about giving me five gold stars.

'Sorry I haven't been to see you for a while, Granny. I've been so busy, trying to sort everything out.'

This time I hear her more clearly. 'Kayla darling, I'm just thrilled that you're out there, leading your wonderful life. That's exactly as it should be.'

Something's still bugging me: Granny's note and necklace are still a puzzle. But now's the perfect time to find out. 'Granny, can I ask you something tricky?'

'Of course, sweetheart.' She sounds drowsy.

'OK here goes. You know your wardrobe –'

She doesn't reply, so I battle on: 'Well, I went in there for a school project, and I found two secret things...'

Silence.

'Granny? Granny? You still there?'

'Hello?' says another voice. 'This is Nurse Kindly. I'm afraid that Mrs Grub's fallen asleep, so we need to end this call. I do hope you understand. Perhaps try again in the morning? Goodbye.' The phone line goes dead.

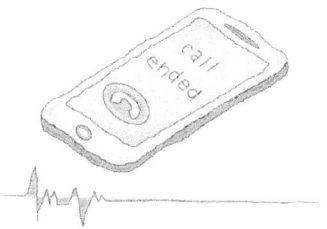

CHAPTER 74

All Ready

It's early on Friday morning and my house is already buzzing. I don't know who's more excited: me about the teachers' job swap, or Mum and Dad about starting their new jobs.

I don't have time to call Granny just yet, because I'm busy making a banner for Mum and Dad. It was going to say 'good luck', but I get carried away and write 'WELCOME TO THE BEST DAY EVER!' Cleo helps me make it by breaking my glitter gun, tripping over my scissors and getting my glue bottle stuck to her paws. I hang up the banner in the living room, as a surprise.

Dad sees it first. 'How lovely!' he says, giving me a hug of pure happiness. He takes his brand new *Head Caretaker* badge from the mantelpiece, gives it a final polish, and proudly pins it to his freshly ironed overalls.

Mum appears at the top of the stairs in her new dinner lady outfit: a full-length apron and matching hat. She's done her hair specially, and looks a million dollars. 'Oh Krystal,' smiles Dad. 'As beautiful as the day we married.'

'You're not so bad yourself, Mr Grub,' she grins, brushing a speck of dust from his overalls and polishing his badge yet again. They go all gooey with each other, so I cough – 'a-hem!' – to make Mum look at the banner. 'Oh, how kind you are, Kukoo!' she says, finally pulling away from Dad to kiss my forehead.

I arrive at school just as Snoop's car sweeps through the front gate. This time, he can't park in Miss Skipper's space, because she's beaten him to it. He gets his own back by parking right behind her, so she can't get out. And when he climbs out, he makes sure he kicks over the *Headteacher* parking sign.

'Woah! Did you see that?' exclaims Milly, running over to join me. 'He's well out of order!'

'Yeah, Dad spent ages fixing that sign back up. He's gonna go mental.'

Dad must have seen it for himself, because he comes rushing out in a rage. 'Excuse me Sir, that type of behaviour is simply not tolerated at Clods, and –'

'Oh not you again,' snaps Snoop. 'I'll report you to the Head Caretaker!'

'You're looking at him,' replies Dad, pointing to his badge.

'Huh! Since when?'

'Today onwards.'

Snoop prods the badge with his finger. 'Well enjoy it while it lasts, my friend. Because by the time I'm finished today, you won't have a job at all.'

'I... I beg your pardon?' stammers Dad.

'Just you wait and see!' snarls Snoop, marching off to the main door.

But he doesn't get far, because Miss Skipper's blocking his way. 'Good morning, Inspector!' she beams. 'And welcome back to Clods! I trust your bank account is nicely topped up? I trust your computer hacking skills are up to scratch? I trust you're well on your way to becoming a Deputy Head?'

'I... I beg your pardon?' he stammers, just like Dad a few moments ago.

'Oh Inspector Snoop, I think we understand one another perfectly well. Since your last visit, I've learnt so much about you!'

He breaks into a sweat and fiddles with his tie pin. 'How? Where? When?'

She ignores his questions. 'At this point, I simply ask one thing: when you inspect my teachers today, you don't go out of your way to destroy them. I don't expect any special favours; just a fair chance. Do I make myself clear?'

'Yes, Miss Skipper. Of course, Miss Skipper,' he murmurs, mopping his brow. She stands aside to let him pass and he staggers into the building. Milly and I throw our arms round each other. 'It's working! It's working!'

Trixie bounces up to us, ready to join in the hug. 'Hi Kayla. Hi Milly. Good to see you both. How ya doin'?'

'Excuse me?' we exclaim, pulling away.

Trixie reaches out to us again. 'What's wrong? Aren't we friends anymore?'

'Friends?' explodes Milly. 'When were you ever friends with a Frizz-Face? Or a Gut-Bucket?'

'What hurtful names!' frowns Trixie. 'Whoever used them wants shooting! Fancy a bag of crisps, by the way? I've got plenty.'

I pull Milly to one side. 'Remember it's all an act! The Grimbag told her to keep us sweet. But only for a few days.'

Milly nods and turns back to Trixie. 'If you think that your pathetic little crisps can bring us round, then you don't know us at all!'

Trixie's only answer is to scramble around in her bag and pull out a multipack. 'What flavour would you both like? Cheese 'n' onion? Barbecue beef?'

I toss my head, scornfully. 'Save your breath. You're wasting your time!'

But it's too much for Milly. 'Ooh, Smoky bacon!' she grins, 'Don't mind if I do!'

Trixie smirks with triumph, but I don't want to fall out with Milly in front of her, so all I can do is roll my eyes.

'Nice!' Milly tells her, crunching away happily. 'Super-smoky, with a strong bacon undertone. Any chance of a second pack?'

'All yours!' gloats Trixie, handing it over.

OK, so Trixie's won the crisp war, but she doesn't realise that we're winning the biggest battle of all. She's got no idea that Miss Skipper's discovered the Dirty Big Secret, or that our teachers have swapped back again. If all goes to plan today, those crisps will seem like nothing at all.

R–ing! Ri–! R–! Time for our first lesson. The next few hours will decide everything.

CHAPTER 75

Out-Snooped

First it's maths, and Snoop's lurking in the corner with his clipboard – just like before. But this time he looks haunted. His latest encounter with Miss Skipper has really shaken him up. When Trixie tries to whisper something to him, he crossly shoos her away. That shakes her up, too: she slips to the back of the class, nervously biting her nails.

The other kids are expecting Mr Props, but Mr Figger walks in, instead. 'Morning everyone,' he begins cheerily. 'I'm sure you're wondering what I'm doing here. The answer's simple: Mr Props and I have swapped jobs. From now on, I'll be teaching you maths and Mr Props will be teaching you drama. Any questions?'

There's a murmur of excitement from the class. Snoop mops his brow. 'OK then,' smiles Mr Figger. 'Let's take it from the beginning.'

He spends the lesson showing us why maths matters. Apparently it explains loads of things - from Coke bubbles, to cobweb patterns, to bus timetables. You name it, and it's got maths behind it. He gets us to try out some of his ideas, and we do maths without even realising.

Trixie tries to catch him out by asking him to calculate the weight of the moon. But he actually shows us how to do it! With proper diagrams and sums and everything!

'Y'know what, Sir?' Milly tells him. 'I always thought that maths was just a load of old numbers. But when *you* do it, it's not so boring.'

'Thank you, Milly,' he laughs. 'I'll take that as a compliment.'

Snoop looks furious: he scribbles away on his clipboard, muttering to himself. I wish I could sneak a look, but he slinks out of the room, halfway through. I just hope that his muttering is a good sign.

R–ing! Ri–! R–! It's the mid-morning break, and Milly's already hungry. 'That's the problem with maths being so mind-blowing,' she grumbles. 'The calories go straight to my brain. Come on, Kayla: let's go grab a snack.'

Today's snack bar is being run by Mum. And now that she's a dinner lady, she's running it her way. For a start, she's making everyone queue properly instead of pushing each other out of the way. She's even making them say 'please' and 'thank you'.

It's all going brilliantly until Snoop barges to the front of the queue and snatches up a doughnut. 'How much?' he snarls at her, opening his wallet. Mum waves her finger at him. 'I've got news for you, Sir: I won't allow that kind of behaviour in my snack bar.'

He recovers from his surprise and inspects her more closely. 'I might've known. You're the Washer-Upper I had the misfortune to meet last time round. You had the cheek to stop me taking extra custard!'

Trixie and the Minx Mob snigger, but Mum looks him straight in the eye. 'I was *Chief* Washer-Upper, if you please. And now I'm a Dinner Lady who won't stand for rudeness. So I'll thank you to return that doughnut to me and go to the back of the queue.'

He stands put, defiantly clutching the doughnut to his chest. It's spilling sugar all over his suit, but he's too worked up to care.

Miss Skipper appears. 'Problem, Inspector?' she asks him, calmly. This punctures him like a pin in a balloon: he hands the doughnut back to Mum and tries to laugh it off. 'My apologies, Miss Skipper. Just a little misunderstanding with your excellent Dinner Lady here. All sorted now.'

'Glad to hear it, Inspector,' she replies. 'And since you no longer need that doughnut, perhaps you'd like to wipe that sticky sugar off your hands?' She hands him a tissue and everyone except Trixie laughs at him.

R–ing! Ri–! R–! Next it's art, and instead of Miss Zinc we've got Mr Kulla. He ignores Snoop in the corner and rolls up his sleeves, keen to begin. 'Listen up, folks: from now on, Miss Zinc will be teaching you science. Yes, we've swapped jobs. Which makes me your new art teacher. Questions?'

'Is it legal to swap jobs?' demands Trixie. 'If not, I'll need to report you!'

Mr Kulla chuckles at the thought. 'Don't worry, Trixie: it's perfectly legal. No need to contact Head Office. Why not try something more productive – like thinking about art?'

Everyone laughs at Trixie – even the Minx Mob. Snoop takes out a couple of headache pills and gulps them down.

Now Mr Kulla's striding up and down, full of energy. 'This term's topic: art that comes from the heart. Please start by drawing a feeling. Don't worry about making it neat and tidy; it's the feeling that's important.'

Trixie sulks in the corner, but the rest of us do pretty well. Our drawings are wild and creative and we're proud when Mr Kulla pins them up on the wall.

Milly's is a bit of a cheat, because she fills her page with the word 'HUNGRY'. But at least the letters are made up of cake, and she's thrilled when Mr Kulla praises the colour of the sponge.

Snoop scowls at everything, but doesn't interfere. He scribbles some more notes, then creeps away before the lesson's finished.

'Where's he off to?' whispers Milly. 'Looks like he's up to something.'

That gets me thinking. What if he's going to inspect every single teacher, to try and find a bad one? What if some of them aren't so good, after all?

I spend the rest of the day sneaking out of class, so I can snoop on Snoop. Each time, a simple sneezing fit is all it takes to buy me five minutes out of the classroom. That's long enough to track Snoop down, and peep through the little window in the classroom door.

I shouldn't have worried. Every time I look, Snoop's watching the best lessons, ever:

* In Mrs Hacker's computer class, they're creating a Clods YouTube channel.
* In Mr Platter's cookery class, they're making a five-tier wedding cake and decorating it with sugar flowers.
* In Miss Zinc's science class, they're using a spotlight and water spray to create a rainbow, spanning across the room.

No wonder Snoop looks like he's swallowed something nasty. Trixie's in a bad way, too: she's bitten her nails off and started chewing her sleeve.

R–ing! Ri–! R–! It's home time, and Milly's still grumbling. 'Honestly, Kayla: I've never had such a hungry day. My brain's whirring so much, I can't get the food in fast enough. This never happened when our teachers were rubbish.'

'But Mills, d'you think we've passed Snoop's inspection? Is Clods safe again? And what about Swindel? Will the Grimbag get booted out?'

'Good point. Amazing what I forget when my tummy's rumbling.'

We've reached the front gate, but we can't get through because it's blocked by a large crowd, thronging around a stage. The whole of Clods and Swindel seems to be here, and half the town too. The crowd's becoming bigger and noisier by the minute.

What's going on?

CHAPTER 76
Press Gang

Milly and I wriggle through the crowd, until we reach the front. Now we're standing in a line of journalists. Some of them have cameras; others have microphones or notepads. The stage looks ready for some kind of celebration. There's masses of bunting, and a giant bottle of champagne, ready to be opened.

Trixie's voice bellows out from the back of the crowd. 'Let me through, you morons!' She elbows her way to the front, and spots us at once. 'Frizz-Face and Gut-Bucket! I might've known you two would be here. Hovering around like a bad smell.'

'Nice to see you too,' sighs Milly. 'Guess you don't wanna be friends, after all.'

'Oh Gut-Bucket, did you really think that those crisps meant anything? Can't believe you fell for it.'

'What if I did? I know better now, and I still got to enjoy two packs of Smoky Bacon!'

I don't hear the rest of their scrap, because I'm listening to the journalists. 'Any idea what this is about?' one of them asks.

'Wish I knew!' says another, 'I just got a message from some bloke I'd never heard of. He promised me a juicy news story if I turned up.'

'Same here. Was your guy called Snoop?'

'Yeah, that's the one. Inspector Snoop.'

Milly grabs me. 'You OK, Kayla? You look like you've seen a ghost.'

'Mills, this whole event's been set up by Snoop!'

'Really? Why?'

'I remember now. Last week, he told Miss Skipper that he'd summon the journalists and tell everyone about Clods being taken over by Swindel. So this show can only mean one thing: he's gonna trash us, after all!'

'Outrageous! Our teachers were brilliant today!'

'Yep.'

'And he promised Miss Skipper to mark 'em fairly!'

'Yep.'

'Oh Kayla, that's JUST NOT FAIR!'

'Whoever said that life was fair?' smirks Trixie. 'Welcome to the real world! A world run by Mum and Snoop and me!'

The Grimbag steps onto the stage and Snoop trails after her, clutching his clipboard. The crowd hold up their phones, ready to film the action. The show's about to begin.

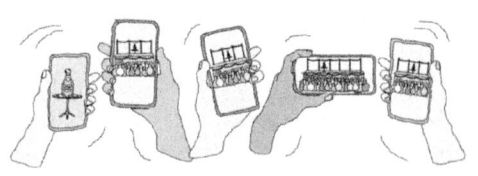

CHAPTER 77

News Flash

The Grimbag loves the attention. She's wearing a bright red suit with extra-sharp shoulders, and her nails are painted to match. Her high heels click like bullets and her collar's so tight, it's pointing up in the air.

She strides to the front of the stage, grabs a mike, and breaks into a dazzling smile. 'Greetings, all! It gives me great delight to introduce myself. I'm Mrs Grimm, Head of Swindel School, where I'm proud to say it's all work, no play!'

Trixie claps and whoops but everyone else is stunned into silence. Snoop's one of the silent ones.

'What's up with him?' whispers Milly. 'Why isn't he cheering her along?'

He doesn't look happy at all. In fact he's sweating buckets, like he's caught in a nightmare. He keeps trying to grab the mike from the Grimbag, but she swats him away, determined to finish her speech.

'Back OFF, Snoopy! Sorry about that, everyone. I'm here to announce some sad news about another school not so far from here. And –'

Snoop finally snatches the mike and addresses the crowd. 'She's wrong! There's no sad news. In fact there's no news at all. So please will you all just GO HOME!'

'But you invited us here!' shouts one of the journalists. 'You told us to expect an announcement!'

Snoops squirms some more. 'I did try to cancel, but I was too late. I couldn't reach Mrs Grimm.'

'I was out of contact!' she hisses at him. 'Have *you* ever tried to answer the phone, while you're having your nails done?'

Trixie groans but everyone else leans forward, more curious than ever.

'What's wrong with the lot of you?' Snoop yells at them. 'Stop gawping and go away!'

The Grimbag tries to grab the mike back again. 'Give it HERE, you thick-witted chump! Of course there's some sad news about that school – and I'm going to announce it, even if it kills me!'

They both tug at the mike, grunting like pigs. It slips through Snoop's fingers and the Grimbag flies backwards. WHACK! Still gripping the mike, she lands on her back with her legs in the air. The crowd surges forward and the cameras zoom in for the best shot.

'Oops!' giggles Milly. 'Those photos are gonna show parts of the Grimbag we've never seen before.'

'And never wanted to see.'

'Yeah. From now on, every time I think of the Grimbag, I'll think of her great big red-knickered b–'

She's drowned out by the crowd's laughter. Snoop's trying to help the Grimbag to her feet, but she thinks he's trying to steal the mike, so she stuffs it down her shirt.

Someone shouts 'These jokers should be on the stage!' Someone else calls out 'They already are!' and the laughter bursts out, louder than ever. Trixie's muttering something savage. It sounds like 'How dare she? She's totally lost it! I'll never forgive her!'

The Grimbag finally pulls herself back up. Her stiff collar has gone floppy but she pulls the mike out of her shirt and restarts her announcement. 'Ladies and gents, please ignore that silly little blip. Now let's get back to that very sad news.'

The crowd simmers down and the Grimbag continues her speech. 'Clods College has just had an official inspection and I'm sorry to say that the results are shockingly bad. I'm now going to share those results with you.' She holds out her hand so that Snoop can pass her the clipboard, but he hides it behind his back, shaking his head.

'Give me the clipboard, you half-brain!' she hisses. He shakes his head again, terrified. She darts behind him to grab it but he holds on tight. They begin their second wrestling match, only this time they tumble off the back of the stage and disappear from view.

The crowd cheers again. 'I wouldn't miss this for the world!' laughs the journalist next to us. Trixie screws her eyes shut and starts humming a tune, to try and get through it.

The Grimbag climbs back onto the stage. She's got hold of the clipboard but she looks like she's come off a battlefield: her pointed shoulders are flattened, her lipstick's smudged across her cheek, and her hair's sticking out like the spikes on a hedgehog. She sets off to the front of the stage, hobbling crazily because one of her high heels has snapped off.

'Y'know what?' says Milly. 'I never thought I'd say this, but I almost feel sorry for her. Some girls just don't know when they're beaten.'

'True,' I sigh. 'You've gotta admire her pluck.'

'Pluck?' grimaces Trixie, opening her eyes again. 'She's a total embarrassment! I'm disowning her. Trixie Grimm's dead and gone. From now on, I'm Trixie Minx, the orphan.'

The Grimbag waves the clipboard in the air. 'Here you have it,' she announces. 'The official record of Clods' shameful failure. That's why you'll be thrilled to hear that I'm taking over Clods and merging it with Swindel. A glorious new mega-school of misery, bossed around by me!'

She hands the clipboard to the journalists. 'See for yourselves! Shocking, as I say.'

The journalists glance at the clipboard, looking confused. 'But Mrs Grimm,' one of them shouts out. 'These results say that Clods is outstanding.' 'Exactly,' shouts another. 'Every score is excellent.'

The Grimbag snatches the clipboard back again and looks at it for the first time. Her face changes colour and she trembles from head to foot. 'SNOOPY!' she howls like it's a swear word. 'You complete and utter IMBECILE!'

He climbs back onto the stage, looking like he's been blitzed by a hurricane. His shirt's hanging out, his glasses are dangling from one ear, and those long strands of hair are now drooping down the side of his face. He wrings his hands in despair. 'It's over, Gabbykins! I had no choice. I had to tell the truth!'

'WHAT?!! WHY?!! NO!!!' screeches the Grimbag, her fierce eyebrows knotting together in the middle of her forehead. This time, they argue in a hissed whisper, and apart from 'Traitor!' and 'Snake!', their words are lost.

Milly and I tear our eyes away and stare at each other. 'Is this for real?' she bursts out.

'Err, yes I think so.'

'Can you pinch me anyway, Kayla, cos I think I must be dreaming.'

We turn to check on Trixie, but she's disappeared. I guess she slipped away when we weren't looking.

Everyone's asking for Miss Skipper, now. 'We'd love you to answer a few questions?' calls out one of the journalists. The crowd parts to let her through, and she walks along the gap, looking straight ahead.

As usual, she's wearing a shabby old suit. Her shoes are scuffed, her blouse is crumpled, and there's a much-used tissue poking out of her sleeve.

For a tiny moment, I can't help wishing that she looked a whole lot smarter. Then I realise that her clothes don't matter, because the crowd only notices one thing: her quiet, impressive confidence.

As she reaches the stage, one of the teachers rescues the mike from the floor and hands it to her. She nods her thanks, switches it on, and turns to face her audience.

CHAPTER 78

Question Time

'Good afternoon, everyone,' she begins. 'I'm sure you're as delighted as I am that Clods is serving our community so well. Special congratulations to our excellent teachers!'

There's a big cheer, then she raises her hand, keen to say more. 'Let's not forget the many others who help to make Clods so special. They're valued every bit as much.'

'Care to name any?' asks one of the journalists.

'Well, what about our wonderful dinner ladies and caretakers, for instance? Today, we salute them too – and our many unsung heroes!'

There's a hearty round of applause, but the journalists aren't satisfied. 'What about Mrs Grimm?' asks one. 'She wanted you to fail. Any idea why?'

Miss Skipper smiles, calm as ever. 'That's a question you'd need to ask Mrs Grimm.'

Other journalists launch in, too. 'What about Snoop?' 'Yeah, why was he acting so fishy?' 'Any thoughts on what he's been up to?'

Miss Skipper cleverly ignores them by appealing straight to the crowd. 'Would any members of the Clods community care to join me onstage? This success belongs to you, so please do come and share it!'

She's soon surrounded by a crowd of teachers, pupils, parents and other well-wishers. The journalists give up their questions and start swapping notes.

Milly pulls me onstage. 'Come on, Kayla: there's no way we're missing this!' She plonks us in the middle of the front row to take some selfies, happier than even crisps can make her.

When the buzz dies down, Miss Skipper takes charge again. 'Another word, if I may. Certain individuals deserve our particular thanks, and I'd now like to name them personally.' She pulls out a list from her handbag, which takes longer than you'd think — because it's sheet after sheet, stuck together.

Milly collapses in a fit of giggles. 'Trust Miss Skipper to make her own toilet roll!'

'Off we go, then,' declares Miss Skipper brightly. 'This will only take an hour or so. First on my list is K—'

WAAHH-WAAHH-WAAHH! She's interrupted by a siren and a flashing blue light. A police car swoops up, and two police officers jump out, ready for action.

'Can we help you?' asks Miss Skipper, as surprised as anyone.

'Thank you, ma'am,' one of them replies. 'We'd like to speak to two of your colleagues. Their names are Grime and Snipe.'

'Grimm and Snoop?' suggests Miss Skipper, pointing to the ragged, bruised couple at the back of the stage. They're still arguing so violently, they only realise what's going on when the police officers charge over and grab them by the arm.

Snoop bursts into tears, but the Grimbag goes on fighting. 'Get OFF me!' she yells at the police officers. 'Low-lifes! Dimwits! Numskulls!'

'Pleased to meet you, too!' they reply, pulling out two sets of handcuffs. 'Now if you'd both like to come with us down to the station?'

'Give us one good reason!' shrieks the Grimbag, trying to pull away. The police officers get serious again. 'We have evidence that you both tried to destroy Clods College. To take it over and exploit it for your own greed. How's that for starters?'

This time, the Grimbag has no answer. As the handcuffs clink shut around her wrists, she stops fighting and lets the police officers lead her and Snoop through the crowd, towards the police car.

The journalists fire off a frenzied round of questions:

>'Any comment on your arrest?'
>
>'How d'you feel about being caught?'
>
>'How many years d'you think you'll be locked away?'

'She made me do it!' blubs Snoop. 'I had no choice! Tell that to the world!'

'He's lying!' growls the Grimbag. 'He's responsible for this! That's your story!'

If only Milly and I hadn't squeezed to the front, to get a closer look. Because when the Grimbag brushes past me, she jolts to a stop. 'That frizzy hair!' she cries out. 'It was you! You stole a boy's uniform and broke into my school!' My body turns to ice and I wonder if I'll ever breathe again.

She leans close towards me, blocking out the light. 'Now I know what you were up to!' she spits. 'You came to sniff out my secrets. You're the one who stuck a knife into my soul! You dirty, meddling witch!'

My legs start to collapse, but Milly props me up.

'Arrest the frizzy girl!' screeches the Grimbag. 'She's pure evil!'

I shut my eyes, ready for the police to handcuff me. But instead of the clink of metal, all I hear is the laughter of the crowd:

'A likely story!'

'The Grimm woman's really lost it, now!'

'Yeah, cracked under the strain!'

When I open my eyes again, the police car is zooming away - with the Grimbag and Snoop still fighting on the back seat.

CHAPTER 79

Backpack Billy

'Well, I guess the show's over,' says one of the journalists, closing their notebook. 'Yeah, but what a show!' says another, packing up their camera. 'It's our hottest story for years. Reckon we'll go viral?'

They stroll out of the front gates, along with the rest of the crowd. After the recent drama, everything's suddenly quiet and empty.

Miss Skipper's standing alone on the stage, still clutching her long 'thank you' list. 'Oh well,' she sighs to herself. 'Perhaps another time.' She stuffs the list into her handbag and heads back into school.

Milly puts her arm round me. 'You look like you could do with a sugar boost. All that excitement has left me low on calories, too. Fancy some chocolate?' She rummages in her bag, but instead of chocolate, she pulls out a piece of paper.

'Hey, what's this? Oh my god, it's a note from Billy! It's been here all day and I didn't even realise!' She scans the page and cries out 'No, no, NO!!!' I grab the note and read it in a flash:

Hey Sis,

By the time you read this I'll be miles away, heading for my new life. I'm going to be a street busker. I've packed a spare set of banjo strings to keep me going. I'm gutted that we'll never see each other again, but I hope you'll be happy.

You and Kayla said that you'll fix Swindel and hopefully you will. But it's too late for me. I can't stand another hour in that prison. And I realise now that Mum will never change her mind.

Hugs,

Bruv

PS. Don't worry about the soggy sleeping bag; I've packed a brolly.

PPS. Say hi to Kayla. I won't forget her.

'He's gone!' sobs Milly. 'Gone for good! And I'll never forgive myself! I should've made Mum listen to him!'

I gulp down my worry and try to stay calm. 'Listen, Mills: we need to find him before it gets dark. With Mum and Dad's help, I'm sure we'll track him down.'

She's crying so much she barely hears. 'He'll never know how much I loved him! And I bet his sleeping bag will get soggy as anything!'

'No it won't!' says Billy, behind us. 'Cos I'm not going anymore.' He's carrying a giant backpack, with his banjo sticking out of the top and his brolly swinging from the bottom.

'BILLY!' she yells, hurling herself at him and thumping his chest angrily.

'Ow!' he protests. 'I thought you actually liked me? Didn't I hear you say so, just now?'

Now she clings onto him like she'll never let him go. 'Idiot! I don't love you one tiny little bit!'

He winks at me over her shoulder, lapping it up, then finally frees himself and puts the backpack down.

Soon, the three of us are sitting on the edge of the stage, sharing the chocolate. 'What made you change your mind?' I ask him, shyly.

'I travelled this way as I headed out of town, and saw the Grimbag and Snoop at each other's throats. That's when I realised they're in big trouble. Which means Swindel will change, after all.'

'Yeah, but who reported 'em to the police?' muses Milly, cramming in three pieces of chocolate at once. 'Was it you, Kayla?'

'No, actually.'

'Miss Skipper, then?'

'Guess so. But when they arrived she looked so surprised. It doesn't make sense.'

Billy chokes on a chunk of chocolate and splutters into his sleeve. 'Billy?' I gasp. 'Was it you?'

'Well what d'you expect?' he chuckles. 'I know I promised to keep the Dirty Big Secret, but when the Grimbag announced her *mega-school of misery*, I finally snapped. That's when I gave the police a call. It felt great, by the way. You can only push a guy so far.'

'Did you give 'em our names?'

'Course not. No names. Just pure tip-off.'

Milly flings her arms round him yet again. 'I'm so glad you did it! Name your reward!'

'A new amplifier for my banjo?'

'The biggest one you like!' she laughs. 'And I won't complain, even when you play flash metal.'

'It's thrash metal, but thanks anyway. Come on: let's go and buy that amp before you change your mind. Coming, Kayla?'

I shake my head. 'You two go ahead. I'm gonna hang around here for a bit.'

'Why? What are you up to?'

'Oh nothing. Just thought I'd wait for Dad to finish work.'

That's another lie (can you spot them by now?). There's someone I want to see, and it's not Dad. The minute Milly and Billy are gone, I head to Miss Skipper's office.

CHAPTER 80

Don't Go

I knock on Miss Skipper's door but no one answers, so I peep inside. She's at her desk, clutching a photo and staring at it like it's her whole world. I recognise the writing on the back: it's the young Pippa and Gabby, when they were still best friends.

When she sees me, she quickly hides it away. 'How nice to see you, Kayla. I thought that you'd be out celebrating with the others.'

'Nah. Thought I'd check on you instead, Miss. Can't be easy seeing your little sister led away by the police.'

'Thank you, Kayla. That's kind of you. But something else is bothering you - I can tell.'

There's no point trying to deny it; she understands me even better than Cleo, and in any case my blush has given me away. 'Remember the Clods Club, Miss? The one you mentioned yesterday, at the staff meeting?'

'Indeed I do. And I hope you recall that you're one of its very first members.'

'Yeah, thanks for that. It felt super-special. But I've decided to resign.'

'Indeed? May I ask why?'

'That club's for people who can make Clods better.'

'And you think you don't qualify?'

'Dead certain, Miss. Cos when I set off the fire alarm, I did some other bad things that you don't know about.'

'Hiding in the lost property cupboard?' she replies starkly. 'Escaping through the window? Flattening my rosebush?'

Her gaze seems to burrow into my head, making it spin. 'How d'you know, Miss? Are you a mind-reader?'

'No, Kayla. I simply thought it through.'

'Miss, I'm dead sorry about the rosebush. But that's not the end of it. I did other bad things, too.'

'Dressing up as Billy Mobbs to sneak into Mrs Grimm's office and print her note?'

'You sure you're not a mind-reader?'

'Quite sure. I learnt this particular fact from Mrs Grimm herself. As the police led her away, she spotted you and shouted a number of accusations. Something about stealing a boy's uniform and breaking into her school.'

'Oh yeah. Awkward.'

'I believed her, even though everyone else laughed it off.'

'Y'know what, Miss? The one time she tries to tell the truth, no one believes her. Bit ironic, really.'

'Ironic indeed. Well spotted, Kayla. I'm impressed!'

She beams at me but it doesn't make me feel any better.

'I suppose it was you who called the police?' she continues. 'I don't blame you, Kayla. I realise now that her crimes had to be reported.'

'Actually, that bit was done by Billy. But he only got involved cos of me. So you see why I can't help with the Clods Club. I have to let it go.' I dig my fingernails into my hands to stop myself crying, but it doesn't work.

She tuts, and I don't know whether it's because she feels sorry for me, or whether she's simply had enough of my snivelling. 'Kayla Grub,' she declares sternly. 'Your resignation is overruled. You are not permitted to resign from the Clods Club. Yes, you've broken our rules. Yes, you've caused damage. But no one's worked harder than you to help Clods succeed.'

She hands me a tissue, which soon gets soggy. I try to flick it into her wastepaper bin, but it flies sideways and splats onto her computer screen. 'Oh god, Miss. I'm sorry!' She tries to stop me going over to pull it free, but it's too late: I've already spotted what she's writing. It's something called *Time to Go*.

'You might as well know,' she states solemnly. 'That's my resignation letter. I'm about to send it to Head Office.'

'You're... leaving?'

'Yes, Kayla. There's a time for everyone to go. My time has come, and I must accept it.'

'But you can't go! You just can't!'

'Kayla, your distress is very flattering, but my mind is made up. You and I both know that I've failed this school. All because of my foolish loyalty to my sister.'

'But isn't that all sorted, now? The teachers are brilliant. The future's bright. You said so, yourself!'

'Yes, the future *is* bright – and you'll be a big part of it. But my days here are over. Clods needs a younger person in the job. A fresh start.' She sits down at her desk and re-reads her letter. Her hand hovers over the mouse, ready to press Send.

How can I convince her to stay? If I don't do it in the next few seconds, it'll be too late. I lean over, snatch up her mouse and keyboard, and clutch them to my chest. 'Sorry Miss, but here's the deal: if you don't resign as Headteacher, I won't resign from the Clods Club. That's my final offer.'

Her frown is almost as severe as the Grimbag's, and she angrily thumps the desk. 'Kayla Grub, you drive an impossible bargain!'

'I've learnt the hard way, Miss. These last few months haven't been easy.'

'Will you at least negotiate?' she scowls.

'No, Miss. The deal won't change.'

She sits back and reads her note again, having a good long think. To my amazement, the corners of her mouth finally twitch into the beginnings of a smile. 'In that case, Kayla, you give me no choice.'

'So you'll... stay?'

'Yes, it seems I will. The Clods Club needs you, after all!'

I think that's the nicest thing anyone's ever said to me.

She glances back at her screen and frowns again. 'Kayla, I'm afraid we still have a problem.'

'Yes Miss?'

'I can't delete the letter without a mouse and keyboard.'

I hand them over and she zaps her letter into nothing. It's replaced by the Clods screensaver - *We Try Our Best* - amid a swirl of brown. That mud-coloured screen makes me laugh and cry at the same time – and now my nose is about to explode. But this time round, she knows better than to hand me a tissue. Instead, she starts scribbling away on a notepad.

'Now Kayla, will you kindly let me get on with it? If I'm staying on as Headteacher, I've got some serious planning to do. The sooner I start, the better!'

I don't budge, and she looks up again with a weary 'Yes?'

'What about Trixie? If Mrs Grimm goes to jail, Trixie will be an almost-orphan.'

'Don't you worry: Trixie's coming to live with me. I've already called her to explain. I know she's bullied you, Kayla, but please don't be too hard on her. She was only trying to please her awful mother. And I'm sure that she'll change, once she's under my roof.'

'OK Miss. It's a truce with Trixie – for now.' I creep out and close the door behind me.

There's one more person I need to speak to: Granny. The second I get home, I take the phone to my room and give her a call. Damn: she's still on voicemail. OK, here goes… 'Hey Granny, your plan worked a treat and everything's sorted! I'll come and see you this evening and tell you all about it. Love you, by the way! Sorry I never said it before.'

I go back downstairs feeling like I've conquered the world. 'Mum? Dad? Are you home? Today has been a blast!'

They're perched on the edge of the sofa, staring into space. 'Hey Mum and Dad, please tell me you saw that crazy stage show, this afternoon? The one with the Grimbag and Snoop and the police and Miss Skipper's long list of thank yous?'

Dad wipes his eyes and speaks softly. 'Kukoo love, I'm afraid we don't know what you're talking about.'

'Don't tell me you missed it? Everyone was there!'

Mum seems a bit weird, too. 'We weren't at school, Kukoo; we were at the hospital.'

My rosy new world melts away in an instant, and I shiver like it's the middle of winter. 'Has Granny got worse?' I whimper. 'Can't she just come home?'

'Darling Kukoo,' they reply, reaching out to me, and sitting me down between them. 'We need to tell you something very sad. Granny's gone, sweetheart.'

My voice goes small and scared. 'Gone where? You mean she's... gone and... died?'

'Yes Kukoo. She died this afternoon.'

'She can't!' I cry out. 'It's too soon! I'm not ready! I still need her!'

'Kukoo sweetheart, there's a time for everyone to go. Granny's time had come. And Granny herself accepted it; she knew she couldn't go on for ever.'

They take my hands and hold them gently. I clench my hands into fists, but they still hold on.

'It was very peaceful, Kukoo.'

'Just before she died, she had a sip of water and asked Nurse Kindly to put your Get Well Soon card onto her pillow, so she could see the picture.'

'Then she drifted into a nice comfy sleep.'

'She never woke up.'

My WELCOME TO THE BEST DAY EVER! banner is still hanging over us, as bright and gleaming as ever.

CHAPTER 81

Granny's Gifts

The Clods victory doesn't matter anymore. Granny's dead and she's never coming back. I'll never be happy again.

After a long chat with Mum and Dad, I go up to my room to break the news to Cleo. I thought she'd be snoozing in her usual spot on my bed, but she's pacing around Granny's room, as if she knows something's wrong.

It's weird to see Granny's stuff exactly where she left it: her slippers by the bed; her dressing gown over the chair; her nightie on the pillow. As if she's just stepped outside for a minute and she's about to charge back in, bursting to tell me one of her funny stories.

I pull Cleo away from pawing Granny's blanket and cuddle her close. 'Hey girl, I know this is hard, but Granny's not inside that blanket, or anywhere else. She's nowhere at all. Unless you reckon she's looking down on us? Do you believe that, Cleo? I guess you'll make up your own mind. You always do.'

What was the last thing I said to Granny, when she actually heard me? It was a few days ago, and I was trying to find out about the note and necklace in her wardrobe. What an idiot! I should've known that it was our last ever time together. I should've said much more important things. But now I'll never get that chance. She didn't even hear my message just now, because she was already dead. I'll never forgive myself.

The next Friday, we take the day off for Granny's funeral. It doesn't feel right to wear black, because Granny clothes were always so bright you needed sunglasses. But Mum says that black is what people expect and sometimes you just have to go along with it. We sit quietly at home, dressed in our weird black clothes, waiting for the taxi to take us to the funeral place.

While we're still waiting, Mum makes a surprise announcement. 'Kukoo darling, your dad and I have come across a couple of things that Granny wanted you to have. We found them when we were sorting through her room. And we agreed that now's a good time to hand them over.'

Dad passes me something wrapped in tissue paper. As it drops into the palm of my hand, it gives a dainty little clink. Yes, it's Granny's necklace: the delicate gold chain, threaded through the tiny gold key. The label's still there, too: *For Kayla.*

'It's gorgeous,' I whisper, holding up the key to the light. 'Any idea what it opens?'

'We were hoping *you* could tell *us*,' says Dad.

'Did Granny ever mention it to you?' asks Mum.

'Nope. Never.'

'Ah well,' she smiles. 'Maybe the key's just for decoration. It's beautiful, after all.'

'Why don't you try it on?' suggests Dad.

'Really? Am I allowed?'

'Of course, sweetheart. It's yours.'

Mum stands me in front of the mirror and carefully arranges the necklace over my black top. 'Oh Kukoo,' she declares softly. 'You look so grown up.'

Dad doesn't say anything but his eyes are shining.

I can't tear my eyes away from my reflection. 'Can I wear it to the funeral? Even though it's not black?'

'Definitely!' smiles Mum. 'Granny would love that.'

'Don't forget the second gift,' says Dad, handing me an envelope. Yes, it's the one I found in Granny's cardigan pocket and the message on the front is as clear as ever: *For Kayla. For when I've gone.*

'Come on then,' says Mum. 'What does it say? We're itching to know!'

They're watching me so intently, I feel shy.
Whatever's in this note, I need to open it when I'm alone.

HONK HONK! A car horn sounds outside. Dad goes over to the window and looks out. 'Taxi's here. Time to go. Ready, folks?'

I drop the note into my pocket. I'll read it when I'm back from the funeral. I've waited so long to know what it says - I'll just have to wait a few more hours more.

Later that afternoon, we're back home, having our tea. We've changed out of our black clothes, but I'm still wearing the necklace. I've got a feeling that I'll be wearing it a lot, from now on. It feels really me.

Luckily, Mum and Dad seem to have forgotten about the note, for now. They're too busy chatting about the funeral.

'How kind of Miss Skipper to come along,' begins Mum, reaching for the teapot. 'She knew about Granny of course, and how much she meant to us. But even so! I was really touched.'

'Me too,' replies Dad. 'Especially when she told us what a strong family we are, and how that's a very precious thing. When she said that, I could've sworn she looked tearful.'

'You're very quiet, Kukoo,' says Mum. 'Anything you'd like to talk about?'

I want to say 'Yes, actually. Why do people have to die?' But it seems pathetic and childish. So instead I say 'Can I take my sandwich up to my room? I think Cleo really needs me, right now. Just the two of us.'

'Of course, sweetheart. Take your time. No rush. And give Cleo our love.'

I climb onto my bed and finish my sandwich, which isn't easy when you're holding a needy cat, who needs a lot of stroking.

It's time to read Granny's note. When I pull it out of the envelope, the first thing I notice is the wonkiness of the lines; they wander across the page like runaway worms. I guess poor Granny was already ill when she wrote it.

Darling Kayla –

I hope that the necklace is now safely in your hands. Have you worked out what the key opens? If not, I'm sure you soon will.

Your very own GG – always and forever.
Xxx

So the key does open something! But what?

I search the whole house, looking for the keyhole. Mum and Dad join in, but we can't find anything. You'd think that Cleo would want to help, but all she does is sit by my bedroom door, meowing.

'There's nothing for that key to open,' says Mum. 'Poor Granny must have got confused.'

'True,' sighs Dad. 'She was very ill, after all. Not her usual self.'

'It's still a beautiful necklace,' I tell them, hating myself for being so disappointed.

CHAPTER 82

Top Story

Over the next few weeks, things start returning to normal. As normal as they can be without Granny. Even though I still miss her loads, I sometimes end up joking around with Milly, or smiling at things online.

At first, when I catch myself feeling happy, I do my best to feel sad again. Then I realise that this would make Granny laugh her head off. After that, I stop trying to feel sad, and allow little moments of happiness to creep up on me.

Cleo stops moping around in Granny's room and rediscovers her knack for knocking my things over, bossing me around and making a nuisance of herself. She's not quite back to normal, though. She still spends hours by my bedroom door, pawing at the panels. She never used to do that before, but I reckon that if I ignore her, she'll eventually give it up.

Anyway, I've got lots of other things to think about. For a start, the school headlines are all over town:

SCANDAL! SWINDEL'S A CON!!! 'We've been duped!' say angry parents.

CLODS IS TOP OF THE CLASS. Exam results are official smarty-pants level!

GRIMBAT AND PIPE-SNIPE face prison. Exclusive interview with insiders who say the duo were always a bit nasty.

I point out this last headline to Mum and Dad. 'Doh! They've got the wrong nicknames. It's the Grimbag and Poop-Snoop.'

'No need to be rude!' Mum warns me. 'However badly they behaved, they don't deserve those spiteful names.'

Dad bursts out laughing. 'The Grimbag and Poop-Snoop? Brilliant!'

Mum rolls her eyes. 'Honestly, Kevin! I give up trying to raise a polite daughter.'

Mum's even crosser when Dad pins up a photo of the Grimbag lying onstage with her legs in the air.

'Come on, Krystal,' he chuckles. 'At least she's wearing proper knickers. You don't see fancy big red ones like that, anymore.'

'How would *you* know?' she sniffs. 'And anyway, the knickers are beside the point. People like us should not be gawping at that kind of photo!'

Dad winks at me, behind her back. I think it would have made Granny laugh, too.

Mum cheers up when she comes across Milly's selfie, showing the two of us smiling in the front row. She puts this one on the mantelpiece, then slaps a label on top with an arrow pointing to me, saying 'Star Pupil'. At least she hasn't put it in the window.

A week later, there's a whole new headline:

CLODS SUPREMO SAVES SCANDAL-HIT SWINDEL. 'I'll do my best to turn it around' says Superstar Skipper.

'Goodness!' exclaims Mum, reading the story. 'Miss Skipper's going to run Swindel as well as Clods! Everyone's asked her to do it: Head Office, the teachers, the parents...'

Dad reads it over her shoulder and calls out to me: 'Hey Kukoo, guess what the real exam results show? Clods has beaten Swindel, year after year! No wonder the Grimbag and Snoop wanted to hide the truth.'

'It's the Swindel kids I feel sorry for,' says Mum. 'All that misery was for nothing. They're the victims, in all this.'

'Just wait till Miss Skipper's in charge!' smiles Dad. 'She'll bring a touch of the Clods magic, eh Kukoo?'

'Yeah, cos our lives have already changed big-time, since we've known her.'

That makes them swap a look that I can't figure out. 'What's up?' I ask them, nervously. 'Something wrong?'

'Don't worry,' begins Dad. 'It's nice news, for a change. It's about money, Kukoo. The fact is, Granny's given us all her savings. She's been very generous.'

'So why are you looking so serious?'

'Because Granny's money gives us choices,' says Mum. 'We don't have to stay here anymore; we can afford to move back to Olding. You can go to Orsum Academy, like you always wanted.'

I leap up in a panic. 'No way! You can't tear me away from Clods or Milly! You'll ruin my whole life! It's just not fair and –' I stop because they're both laughing.

'Kukoo love, we're so glad you said that. Let's stay right where we are. That's just what we want, too.'

CHAPTER 83

Busy Bods

The rest of term is busier than ever. Each teacher's determined to get the best out of us, and we're grappling with big new ideas, every single day. 'Can't we swap the teachers back again?' grumbles Milly. 'I'm so busy expanding my mind, it's cutting into my pony time!'

We're both busy with the Clods Club, too. Loads of people have joined, and each member's in charge of something. I'm setting up a charity bake-off and Milly's running a Christmas show.

Milly comes round for a sleepover whenever her mum's too tired to say 'no'. And when my mum's not looking, we binge on trash-TV and sticky popcorn. We don't even have to worry about the crumbs, because Cleo eats them up, like a furry four-legged hoover.

Apart from missing Granny, life feels pretty good.

Even Trixie doesn't bother us anymore. Now that she's living with Miss Skipper, she leaves us alone. Everyone avoids her anyway, because word's caught on that she's the Grimbag's daughter. We thought that the Minx Mob might stick by her, but they were the first to run off.

'Why doesn't she try to get her mobsters back?' Milly asks me, one day. 'Is she trying to be a better person, or has she simply run out of money for crisps?'

'Dunno, Mills. Maybe we should chat to her, sometimes?'

'You kidding? She made our life a nightmare! Hasn't our big school meltdown taught you anything?'

'Yeah: no one's perfect.'

'Is that it?' she snorts. 'That's all you've learnt?'

I like to think that I've learnt a whole lot more. But I can't put it into words. Not yet, anyway.

Instead, I tell Milly how I felt when I first walked into the Clods playground. 'I was all alone, Mills. I know what "zero friends" feels like. That's why Trixie deserves another chance. What if all her pony-tail swishing is just a front? What if she's more like us than we realise?'

'OK, fine. Let's have one chat with her. But no more. At least not to start with. And not until I've finished my Christmas show!'

Who knows how Trixie will react? Will we find a softer side, lurking underneath? Stranger things have happened.

Ring ring ring! Dad's mended the Clods bell, so it doesn't conk out halfway through. I miss the old one, but I guess you can't have everything.

'Now let's rescue the school sign,' he tells me, disappearing into the bushes where it fell over on the first day of term. He fixes it up, and repaints the slogan in the right shade of brown: *Clods College: We Try Our Best*.

Next, he scrubs at the line that's still scribbled underneath: *But You're Still Rubbish!*

'Any idea who wrote this?' he asks me. I'm sure it's Trixie's handwriting, but I don't say anything. She's been punished enough.

Most of the words disappear, but the *Rubbish* won't budge. Dad adds some new words, so now it reads: *And We Recycle All Our Rubbish!*

'It's true, Kukoo,' he smiles. 'All Clods rubbish now gets recycled, thanks to your mum and me. We're entering Clods for an Eco-School award!'

That afternoon, Milly and I meet up with Billy after school. We get Toffee Waffles and eat them sitting on a wall. 'It's good to escape our house for a bit,' says Billy. 'Mum's worse than ever, now that she's decided to sue the Grimbag and Poop-Snoop.'

'She's doing what?'

Milly grips my arm. 'Oh, didn't I say? She's furious with 'em for pretending that Swindel was a top-scoring school. She's demanding a truckload of money.'

'She'd better not pull me out of Swindel,' warns Billy. 'If she does, I'll protest all over again!'

'So Swindel's now your dream school?' I ask him, amazed at the turnaround.

'Yeah, everything's changed now that Miss Skipper's in charge. Plus there's a guy there who plays the drums, and we're getting a thrash metal band together.'

'With you on the banjo?'

'Of course.'

'What's it called?'

'Crusty Scab,' he mumbles shyly.

299

'Isn't that what your SWINDEL SUCKS message turned into? A crusty scab which then fell off?'

'Y'know what, Kayla? You don't miss a thing!'

Milly laughs so hard, her toffee filling drips all over her skirt. 'Don't worry,' she tells us happily. 'I'll lick it off when I get home.'

'Can I continue?' persists Billy. 'There's another reason to stay at Swindel.'

'The teachers?' I suggest helpfully. 'The indoor swimming pool? The double-length stage?'

'Nah,' he grins. 'Purple suits me better than brown. Don't you think, Kayla?' He's clearly not expecting a reply, because he gives me a funny look and scoots off.

'He likes you!' giggles Milly as soon as he's gone.

CHAPTER 84

Best Ever

Ring ring ring! It's the last day of term before the Christmas holidays, and I'm hurrying to my final lesson.

Miss Skipper appears in her office doorway and calls out to me. 'Kayla Grub! A quick word, if you please.'

Oh no! What have I done wrong? She hasn't spoken to me since we chatted in her office all those weeks ago, just after the Grimbag and Snoop were led away by the police. I've often spotted her dashing around, and wondered how she manages to run two schools so brilliantly. She still wears those crumpled suits and scuffed shoes, but nowadays she has a fresh twinkle in her eye and a spring in her step.

She takes one look at my face and smiles. 'Apologies: I should've explained. This isn't meant to be painful. Quite the opposite.'

What's the opposite of painful? I try to work it out while she goes to her desk, takes a piece of paper, and starts to write.

Her office has changed so much, I hardly recognise it. Someone's put shelves up. Everything's neat, clean and tidy. She glances up and spots me staring around. 'Wonderful, isn't it?' she declares. 'All thanks to your clever father. He helped me to sort myself out.'

The vase of yellow roses is back, filling the room with colour. 'Aren't they beautiful?' says Miss Skipper, still writing. 'Your father replaced the dead rosebush with a lovely new one, so we'll have roses again next summer. Until then, I'm buying them from the florist. My special treat to myself!'

She holds the piece of paper towards me. 'It's a certificate, Kayla. On the last day of term, I like to award these to one or two people who've truly excelled.'

I take it, too surprised to say anything. The paper's Clods-brown and stamped with the school motto, *We Try Our Best*. Underneath, she's written: *Kayla Grub: Best Use of a Swindel Boy's Uniform*. Then there's her signature: a crazy jumble of loops and swirls.

It's the best certificate I've ever had, but something's troubling me.

'Anything wrong?' Miss Skipper asks me, taken aback.

'Sorry Miss, but I couldn't have done it without Milly Mobbs. She helped me every step of the way.'

'I see. Are you telling me that she's earned a certificate, too?'

'She's never had one before, Miss. Not even for pony-riding, which is her best thing. It'd mean so much to her.'

'Very well. If nothing else, Milly does deserve credit for being mad enough to go along with your schemes.' She reaches for another certificate and thinks out loud. 'Ah, but what has Milly done best, I wonder? Pony-riding doesn't count, I'm afraid; it has to be something to do with Clods, and how she's helped us to get back on track. A-ha! Got it.'

She fills in the certificate and hands it over. Her solution makes me smile: *Milly Mobbs: Best Friend*.

'Perfect, Miss! I'm so grateful. I –'

'Yes, yes,' she interrupts. 'But Kayla, from now on there must be no more meddling. Do you understand? And when you become Prime Minister I shall expect an invitation to Number 10.'

'Actually Miss, I'm not gonna be Prime Minister. I'm not gonna do any of those jobs my parents go on about.'

'Indeed? In that case, which career have you chosen? Burglar, Detective – or a combination of the two?'

'I'm gonna be a writer, Miss.'

'Good for you, Kayla. I'd advise plenty of practise.'

'That's the tricky bit, Miss. Dunno where to start.'

'Why not start by writing about yourself? Now there's a story worth telling!'

'But who'd wanna read about me? And who'd ever believe it's true?'

'You'd be surprised. Everyday life is as strange and fruitful as we want it to be. Because we're all making that story happen, even if we never write it down.'

As I think about this, a whole new world starts opening up in my head. But then she glances at the clock and gives herself a shake. 'Now get along with you. I'm now running two schools, don't forget!'

'Yes Miss. Thank you Miss.'

By the time I've reached the door, she's already busy with her paperwork and happily humming away.

CHAPTER 85

At Last

Ring ring ring! The final lesson's over and everyone's heading home for the Christmas break.

I hand over Milly's certificate, and she's beyond thrilled. 'Can you believe it?' she squeals. 'Best friend! At last I'm actually good at something!'

But when I suggest that it'll make her mum proud, the light goes out of her eyes. 'Not true, Kayla: she won't care one little bit. All she's bothered about is getting that stupid money out of the Grimbag and Poop-Snoop. It's still dragging on and she barely notices Billy and me anymore.'

She looks at her certificate and cheers up again. 'I'll keep it in the corner of my bedroom, where Mr Bunnyfun used to live. It'll stop me missing him so much. And whenever Mum says I'm useless, I'll go and look at my certificate and tell myself that she's wrong.'

I wish I could solve Milly's problems, but maybe fixing families is even harder than fixing schools. In the meantime, all I can do is give her a hug. 'Mills, you're the best *everything*! One day, everyone else will know that too.'

I get home to find Mum and Dad waiting for me in the hallway, even though they're still meant to be at work. I stop dead, worried that there's some horrible news. But then they fling open the living room door with a big 'Ta-dah!'

They've decorated the whole place with balloons, just like the day I left Peach Primary. There's even a cake and a line of party-poppers, the same as before. 'We've heard about your new certificate!' they smile. 'Miss Skipper told us, this afternoon. Come on then, Kukoo: let's see it!'

When I hand it over, they're every bit as puzzled as I expected. 'Best Use of a Swindel Boy's Uniform? What does that mean?'

'It was part of a drama class,' I reply. 'You know what Mr Props is like; always coming up with different costumes!'

I hope that's the last lie I have to tell for a good long while. And at least it works, because Mum now beams with pride. 'Well I never! That even beats your triumphs at Peach Primary!'

'But Mum, back then it was just stuff like trampolines and glitter guns.'

'Exactly! Kukoo darling, you've come a long way.'

Dad clearly agrees, because he fires off a handful of party-poppers, whooping along with each BANG. Mum pulls some party-popper strings from her hair and carries on. 'Your dad and I have discussed something else. We'd like to buy you a present to say *well done*.'

'What d'you fancy, Kukoo?' says Dad. 'Whatever it is, you've earnt it!'

I catch my reflection in the mirror and it confirms what I'm going to answer. 'Actually, yes there is something.'

'Sure,' they say eagerly. 'What is it?'

'It's something I've wanted for ages.'

'Even better! What is it?'

'It'll make a massive difference to my life.'

'Kukoo, will you please just tell us? WHAT IS IT?'

'A brand new school uniform that actually fits!'

I take a step back, awaiting their reaction. They're not exactly cross, but they're definitely puzzled.

'What's wrong with your current uniform?' frowns Dad, looking me up and down. 'OK, it got a bit torn recently, but you've mended it well enough.'

'And it'll fit fine, once you grow a bit more,' decides Mum, twirling me round for inspection.

My answer is ready and waiting. I start by unrolling my sleeves until they droop to my knees. Then I unfasten the safety pin, so my skirt hangs down crooked. Finally, I untie my shoes and pull out the scrunched-up balls of newspaper that stop them from slipping off.

Cleo thinks the newspaper balls are a toy, and starts shredding them to pieces. But Mum and Dad don't notice; they're staring with horror at my droopy, crooked, over-sized clothes.

'Oh Kayla,' says Mum quietly. 'I'm so sorry. I'd no idea. Of course you should have a new uniform. Let's go and get it tomorrow.'

'All this time, you kept it secret!' sighs Dad. 'I suppose you didn't want us to worry. Kayla my girl, you're still full of surprises.'

Now it's my turn to be shocked. But it's not about the uniform; it's because of what they've just called me. 'Excuse me? Did you both just say *Kayla*, not *Kukoo*?'

They swap an amazed glance. 'Oh my goodness, so we did!'

Mum turns back to me with a smile. 'After everything that's happened in the last few months, your baby name doesn't seem right anymore.'

'Dead right!' declares Dad. 'It's Kayla from now on.'

Cleo stops shredding the newspaper balls and gazes up at me. There's a new look in her eyes. I think it's called respect. At last.

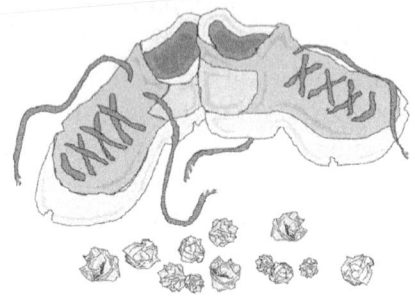

CHAPTER 86

The Key

There *is* a keyhole, of course. Maybe you've already worked out where it is? But it takes me ages to find it, even though I walk past it every day, and Cleo's doing her best to show me. She's never given up sitting by my door, gazing up and pawing at the panels. But I guess I haven't been listening to her like I used to, when I was still Kukoo.

One day, she gets so desperate, she swipes my necklace from my bedside table and scrapes it against the door, jumping as high as she can. 'Hey!' I shout crossly, 'Give that back! It's my most precious thing in the whole world!'

Next, she digs around in my desk drawer, pawing away at the contents. 'Leave it alone!' I snap, tidying it up again. On top, I spot the note that Granny sent me, just before I left Olding. One of its lines catches my eye:

Every door has its own key.

OF COURSE! Why the hell didn't I realise? Clutching the key, I leap over to my door, scouring its surface for a keyhole. When I get to the peephole, Cleo actually turns a somersault. But the key doesn't fit, and now I blame her for leading me on. I call her all sorts of names that I don't even know how to spell.

You'd think this kind of language would put her in her place, but she jumps onto my chest and presses her face so close to mine, her whiskers tickle my nose. That's when I finally hear her again. 'You idiot!' she's yelling. 'Try the peephole on the other side! The side that no one can see through!'

I race onto the landing and do as she says. This time the key fits perfectly, turning with a little 'click'. As if by magic, one of the panels swings open – a door within a door! And inside, there's a book! It's been hidden inside my bedroom door, all this time!

I pull it free, and chuckle at the title that's written on the front: *The Secret Kayla Grub*. Oh Granny, this is your best game, ever.

But every page is blank! How can an empty book be the secret to anything, let alone me?

Cleo has the answer yet again: she leaps back onto my desk, picks up a pen with her mouth, and drops it into my lap. 'So this book's for me to write in?' I ask her, stunned. I guess she's fed up with me being so stupid, because after a single 'Doh!', she settles at my feet and nods off.

I sit there for a long while, pen in hand and blank page in front of me. Remember what Miss Skipper told me, when I said I wanted to be a writer? 'Why not write about yourself?' she said. It's decided, then: I'll tell my own story. All the secrets that I've had to deal with, since my life was turned upside-down. I reckon that Granny would like that, too.

I turn to the first page and write the first few sentences:

Everything in this book is totally true. How do I know? Because it happened to me and then I went and wrote it down.

Over the next few weeks, my story grows and grows. Each time I scribble down more of what happened, I burn with energy, feeling more alive than ever.

At first, I try to glue some extra pages into the book, but the glue comes out in dirty streaks. It's those crushed-up rose petals I was anxious to hide, all those weeks ago. So I give up on gluing extra pages and decide to save space, instead. I simply leave out Cleo's hour-long lectures, and write what's left.

Maybe you're wondering whether I ever finished my story? Well yes I did, actually. Right to the end. Because this is it.

ISBN: 9798877197169
Text and pictures by Kate Eden, typeset by Beck Laxton
© Kate Eden, 2024
Enquiries to *kateedenworks@gmail.com*

Printed in Great Britain
by Amazon